A PASSION FOR FRUIT

A
PASSION
FOR
FRUIT

LORENZA DE'MEDICI

PHOTOGRAPHS BY MIKE NEWTON

PAVILION

First published in Great Britain in 1999 by

PAVILION BOOKS LIMITED

London House, Great Eastern Wharf, Parkgate Road,
London SW11 4NQ

Text copyright © 1999 Lorenza de'Medici
Text with the assistance of John Meis
The moral right of the author has been asserted.

Photographs copyright © 1999 Mike Newton
Home economist: Lisa Heathcote

Designed by David Fordham

A CIP catalogue record for this book is available from the British Library.

ISBN 1 86205 104 6

Colour reproduction by Alliance Graphics
Printed and bound in Spain by Egedsa

10 9 8 7 6 5 4 3 2 1

This book may be ordered by post direct from the publisher.
Please contact the Marketing Department. But try your bookshop first.

All recipes serve 6 unless otherwise stated.

CONTENTS

*'Feed him with apricocks and dewberries,
With purple grapes, green figs, and mulberries'*
SHAKESPEARE, A MIDSUMMER NIGHT'S DREAM, III, i

INTRODUCTION

The word 'paradise' comes from an ancient Persian word originally used to describe the walled fruit gardens and orchards of kings and nobles. In the West it referred to the Garden of Eden, an earthly place of supreme delight, and then became synonymous with heaven, the state of eternal bliss. Unfortunately we were expelled from the Garden of Eden and lost our earthly paradise, but mercifully we are still blessed with gardens and orchards of wondrous fruit to enjoy.

Fresh fruit provides us with one of life's great sensual pleasures. It is beautiful to behold on the branch and on the table, fragrant and aromatic to smell, satisfying to touch, delicious and beneficial to eat. In short, a taste of paradise. We have fallen from grace, however, and live in a world where that pleasure is being eroded. What with the 'world market place', modern technologies and commercial interests, where there are no seasons and everything is available all year round, we are in danger of losing the simple enjoyment of eating a fresh, locally grown piece of sun-ripened fruit. If nothing else I hope these pages encourage you to wait until summer for fresh strawberries and in winter to enjoy your preserves.

Just as the splendid still-life photographs of Mike Newton are Italian in inspiration, so my comments and reflections on fruit are from an Italian perspective. I have also included information that I hope you will find interesting as well as useful. Selecting recipes to go along with these presented a problem I had not foreseen. I found myself writing over and over again, 'This fruit is best enjoyed just as it is, straight from the tree.' All of which is true. Nevertheless, cooking fruit and eating food cooked with fruit provide unique culinary and gastronomic pleasures that allow you to celebrate the arrival of each season with new colours, textures and tastes. I have chosen some of my favourite fruit recipes which I hope will add to your enjoyment in the kitchen and pleasure at the table.

ORCHARD FRUIT

APPLES

(PYRUS MALUS)

APPLES ARE THE PRIMEVAL FRUIT. According to the religious myths of most ancient cultures the apple is sacred in one way or another, the fruit of paradise, promising immortality. So it is especially fitting that botanists discovered the primeval apple forest in Kazakhstan on the slopes of what the Russians call the Heavenly Mountains. Anyone who has had the pleasure of eating a perfect apple off the tree will sympathize with Adam and Eve and agree that there is something divinely tempting about the fruit, its combination of a crisp-juicy texture and tart-sweet taste. I know people who don't particularly like apricots or who could pass up a fig, but who can resist biting into a good apple?

After thousands of years of cultivation, more than 7,500 varieties are grown around the world, making the apple the most highly and widely cultivated fruit there is. It can grow in any climate, except the most extreme, practically the year around, and it comes in all sizes, shapes, colours and flavours. Besides the rounded fruit, some apples are long and cone-shaped, others are short and somewhat flattened. Apple skins come in green, yellow, brown, red, almost purple and nearly black, and some are blushed, streaked, 'russeted', blotched or speckled in combinations of all these colours. Inside they can be golden, pure white or have a greenish tint. Take your first bite out of a Pink Pearl and you will be pleasantly shocked by its pink flesh. Some apples are crisp and crunchy to the bite, others smoother and more tender. They can be tart, tangy, sweet or spicy and, as befits this archetypal fruit, some varieties have an aroma or taste reminiscent of other fruits, like the banana (the Winter Banana) and grape (the Winesap).

Unfortunately not many of us, unless we live in certain parts of England, France or the United States, are able to enjoy even a small taste of this horticultural wealth at our local markets or greengrocers. The demands of the contemporary consumer for picture-perfect fruit and the difficulties of industrial apple cultivation – to kill off pests and diseases commercial orchards spray their trees and fruit with toxic chemicals several times a year – have all but eliminated from common commerce many of the most delicious fruits from our ancient apple heritage. And worse is already on its way: genetic engineering on the apples of the future. On the bright side young growers in every part of the world are carrying on the tradition of cultivating local varieties and reviving 'heritage' antique apples.

Of the relatively few we are left with that can be universally and easily found, only a dozen or so varieties, a good Cox's Orange Pippin is probably the best all purpose apple. Its mellow, aromatic flesh has good flavour for eating fresh and the solid texture necessary for cooking. I think the Gravenstein, which is said to be of Italian origin, is the best apple for baking.

APPLES WITH BRAISED RED CABBAGE

1 SMALL WHITE ONION, PEELED AND
CHOPPED
3 TBSP EXTRA-VIRGIN OLIVE OIL
1 KG/2¼LB RED CABBAGE, CORED AND
VERY THINLY SLICED
6 COX'S APPLES, PEELED, CORED AND
QUARTERED
SALT AND PEPPER

In a large pan, fry the onion in the olive oil until it is translucent. Add the cabbage and cook, covered, over a low heat until it is soft, about 1 hour, adding a little water when necessary to keep it moist. Add the apples and cook for 10 minutes more. Adjust the seasoning with salt and pepper and stir well. Serve hot, perhaps with venison or lamb.

APPLE AND MINT SORBET

MAKES APPROXIMATELY
1 LITRE/1¾ PINTS
2 KG/4½LB GRANNY SMITHS, PEELED,
CORED AND QUARTERED
4 TBSP WATER
1 HANDFUL FRESH MINT LEAVES OR
2 TBSP DRIED MINT
240G/8OZ/1 CUP SUGAR
4 TBSP CALVADOS

Slice the apple quarters into a saucepan. Add the water and the mint, then cook, covered, stirring occasionally, until soft, about 5 minutes. Discard the fresh mint, if you are using it, then add the sugar and stir until it has dissolved. Purée the apple mixture in a blender. Let it cool slightly, add the Calvados and mix well. If you have an ice-cream maker, freeze the sorbet according to the manufacturer's instructions. Otherwise, pour the sorbet mixture into a bowl and put it into the freezer for at least 4 hours to set. After the first 30 minutes, take it out and whisk it to break up the ice crystals, then return it to the freezer. Whisk twice more at half-hourly intervals, then leave the sorbet to become firm.

APPLE AND RICE DUMPLINGS

480 ML/16FL OZ/2 CUPS MILK
240G/8OZ/1 CUP ARBORIO RICE
120G/4OZ/½ CUP SUGAR
4 COOKING APPLES
1 TSP POWDERED CINNAMON
3 LARGE EGGS
90G/3OZ/¾ CUP PLAIN (ALL-PURPOSE)
FLOUR
1 LITRE/1¾PT/4 CUPS OIL
30G/1OZ/2 TBSP ICING-SUGAR

Put the milk into a saucepan and bring it to the boil. Add the rice and cook, stirring, over a low heat until it is tender, about 18 minutes. Add the sugar, stir, and leave it to cool to room temperature. Peel, core and grate the apples, then add them to the rice with the cinnamon. Separate 2 of the eggs and add the yolks to the rice mixture. Beat the whites and lightly fold them in. Beat the remaining egg lightly on a plate. Form the rice mixture into balls the size of large walnuts, then dip them in the beaten egg and coat them with the flour. Heat the oil in a deep-fryer to175°C/350°F, or use a large cast-iron saucepan, and cook the apple and rice dumplings in it a few at a time for about 5 minutes until they are golden. Drain on absorbent kitchen paper, then dust with the icing-sugar. Serve immediately if possible, although they will keep hot for up to 10 minutes in a warm oven with the door left ajar.

PEARS

(PYRUS COMMUNIS)

'*You should go to a pear tree for pears, not to an elm.*'
(PUBLIUS SYRUS, SENTENTIAE)

PEARS ORIGINATED IN ASIA MINOR and like apples, to which they are related, grew wild in prehistoric times. Over the centuries horticulturists developed two different species of pear: the European and the Asia, both still thriving today. Ancient Roman botanists had already classified over fifty different types of the European species and by Renaissance times the Medici gardeners were cultivating some two hundred kinds of pear. The story goes that a variety which was to become famous, the William, was introduced into France by San Francesco di Paola who had brought it with him from Calabria to the court of Louis XIV. Because of Louis XIV's insatiable appetite for the pear it became the favoured fruit of the court and soon the gardeners of Versailles were developing new and ever more flavourful varieties. Today over five thousand types of pear are known, although only a dozen or so are commercially cultivated. Italy is the largest producer of pears in Europe, most of them for juice.

Some varieties of pear begin to ripen towards the end of July and others continue through autumn into early winter. Picking pears at the right time is tricky and so is choosing them at the market. Unlike most orchard fruit, pears ripen from the inside out so if you wait for them to ripen on the tree before picking, the inside will be mushy. They have to be picked while still underripe but not before the stem snaps off when the fruit is gently twisted. Then they are left to ripen off the tree. As soon as a pear is ready to eat it goes over the top quickly. Unless you are going to eat them almost the same day, it is better to buy fruit that is a little underripe and keep it at home for several days until it is ready. You can tell when a pear is perfectly ripe if the flesh near the stem gives slightly to the touch.

Pears come in numerous shapes and colours and go by different names in different countries. However, I have found that most pear-eaters will prefer either the soft, buttery, sweet and juicy kind of pear, like the Anjou or Bartlett (the William), or the firm, crisp, granular and slightly acidic varieties like the Roche or Forelle.

Pears are a lovely fruit for a salad and good in desserts. The celebrated chef, Escoffier, served them with vanilla ice-cream, warmed with a dark chocolate sauce in his famous recipe, Poires Belle-Hélène. An old Tuscan adage warns the landlord not to let his tenant share-cropper find out how good pears taste when eaten with pecorino, sheep's milk cheese – or run the risk of getting less of both when the time comes for the farmer to turn over his share of the produce. Like all folk wisdom this saying was obviously thought up by the peasant farmer. The joke was on the *padrone*.

POACHED PEARS WITH CARAMEL SAUCE

6 COOKING PEARS, PEELED, HALVED
AND CORED
120G/4OZ/½ CUP SUGAR
6 TBSP RED WINE
240ML/8FL OZ/1 CUP DOUBLE (HEAVY)
CREAM

Put the pears in a saucepan with half of the sugar and the wine, cover, and cook over a low heat until tender, about 10 minutes. Drain the pears, reserving the juices, and arrange them on a plate. Put the rest of the sugar into a small saucepan and bring it to the boil, stirring until the sugar has dissolved. Continue to boil, without stirring, until it has caramelized – a drop poured on to a plate will harden within a few seconds. Add the reserved juices. Beat the cream until soft peaks form, then fold it into the caramel sauce. Spoon the sauce over the pears and serve.

PEAR TARTE TATIN

90G/3OZ/6 TBSP UNSALTED BUTTER
90G/3OZ/6 TBSP SUGAR
4 COOKING PEARS, PEELED, HALVED
AND CORED
1 DISC PUFF PASTRY, 23CM (9IN)
DIAMETER, DEFROSTED IF FROZEN

Preheat the oven to 200°C/400°F/gas mark 6.

Take a 23-cm (9-in) tart tin and cover it with the butter. Sprinkle over the sugar. Arrange 6 of the pear halves with the pointed ends towards the centre and the rounded side down. Slice the remaining 2 pear halves and use them to fill in the gaps.

Lay the tart tin on the hob and cook over a low heat until the sugar and butter start to caramelize and become golden. Remove it from the heat and leave it to cool. Cover the pears with the puff-pastry disc and prick it all over with a fork. Bake for about 30 minutes or until golden brown. Allow it to cool completely. Just before serving, return the tart tin to the hob and turn up the heat high. Leave it for a few minutes until the caramel has melted. Now invert the tart quickly on to a plate – but be very careful not to burn yourself on the hot juices. Serve warm.

PEAR TARTLETS

360G/12OZ PUFF PASTRY, DEFROSTED
IF FROZEN
2 COOKING PEARS, PEELED, HALVED
AND CORED
2 TBSP PEAR LIQUEUR (E.G. POIRE
WILLIAM)
30G/1OZ/2 TBSP SUGAR
1 TBSP WATER
30G/1OZ/2 TBSP UNSALTED BUTTER

Preheat the oven to 200°C/400°F/gas mark 6.

Roll out the pastry and cut into 6 circles, each one roughly 10cm (4in) in diameter. Place on a baking sheet and prick the pastry all over with a fork. Slice the pears thinly lengthwise and lay them slightly overlapping on the pastry circles. Bake for 25 minutes. Remove from the oven and brush the pears with the liqueur. Meanwhile, put the sugar and water into a small saucepan over a medium heat. Dissolve the sugar, then boil until just before it starts to caramelize. Take the pan off the heat, stir in the butter and brush the pears with the sauce. Serve warm.

I was given this lovely recipe by Altoplato, the cooking school in Milan and it has been a pleasure to serve to friends over the years.

APRICOTS

(PRUNUS ARMENIACA)

'*Who doubts you sweet*
With savoury almond-stones,
Apricots?
When you were young
You had star flowers,
Now you are little suns
Ripe in the leaves.'
(LEYEL, THE GENTLE ART OF COOKERY, 1947)

I DON'T KNOW EXACTLY WHY, but every time I eat a dried apricot or taste apricot preserves during the winter, it feels like I just popped a little sunshine into my mouth. Maybe it is the warm golden colour of the fruit or maybe it is because the apricot is the first fruit tree to blossom in early spring and kindles hope for sunny days ahead. The Persians called apricots 'seeds of the sun', and the ancient Greeks 'golden eggs of the sun', so my sensation seems universal.

The late Latin name for this fruit from which the English 'apricot' is derived was praecoquus, meaning precocious or early-ripening. Unfortunately apricots are too precocious for their own good and they are often nipped in the bud by a late frost. In northern Tuscany where I live we barely begin to enjoy their lovely blossoms before some cold, wet wind ruins our pleasure.

As a result the fruit that survives is often harvested too early and arrives in the market underripe, still a little hard. A sun-ripened apricot isn't ready for picking until midsummer. By then it has turned a colour so uniquely beautiful it is called after itself, apricot, a glowing yellow orange with a rosy flush. The skin is velvety and the fruit has a fabulous fragrance. The flesh is not juicy, nor is it dry, but rather firm and meaty, deliciously flavourful and sweet to the taste.

I know a tree in a friend's garden where I can sometimes eat them as perfect as this, still warm from the sun, but it is a rare treat. Fortunately, given the delicate constitution of apricots, they are excellent dried. Once, from an aeroplane about to land in San Francisco, I saw colourful sheets of them laid out in the sun on the hillsides of orchards in San Jose, California. A delicious and simple way to prepare dried apricots is to soak them overnight in Vin Santo: a strong, sweet Italian dessert wine. Freshly cooked and preserved apricots add flavour and a suggestion of the exotic East to both savoury and sweet recipes.

APRICOT CHUTNEY

MAKES 600G/1¼ PINTS
120G/4OZ DRIED APRICOTS
500G/1LB FRESH APRICOTS, HALVED
1 HANDFUL DARK RAISINS
1 TBSP GROUND ALLSPICE
6 CLOVES
500ML/16FL OZ/2 CUPS RED WINE
VINEGAR
240G/8OZ/1 CUP SUGAR
2 APPLES, PEELED, CORED AND
GRATED

Wash the dried apricots and put them in a bowl. Cover them with water and leave them to stand until they are soft, for about 1 hour. Drain them and chop them roughly. Put the fresh apricots into a saucepan with the softened dried ones, add the raisins, the allspice, the cloves, the vinegar, the sugar and the apples and cook over a very low heat, covered, for about 2 hours, until the mixture is dark and the liquid has evaporated. Have ready some sterilized warmed jars, fill them with the chutney and seal them. They will keep like this in the refrigerator for up to 2 weeks. If you wish to store the chutney for up to a year, fill the warmed jars with the chutney, seal them tightly, then put them in a saucepan and cover them with water. Bring it to the boil and cook for 25 minutes. Turn off the heat and let the jars cool completely in the water. Then remove them and store them in a cool, dark place.

PORK LOIN WITH APRICOTS

1.5KG/3¼LB PORK LOIN
SALT AND PEPPER
30G/1OZ/2 TBSP UNSALTED BUTTER
2 TBSP EXTRA-VIRGIN OLIVE OIL
600G/1LB APRICOTS
9 AMARETTI (ALMOND BISCUITS),
CRUMBLED
90G/3OZ/⅔ CUP ICING-SUGAR
1 LARGE EGG

Preheat the oven to 200°C/ 400°F/gas mark 6.

Season the pork with plenty of salt and pepper. Melt the butter and oil in a roasting-tin and put in the pork. Place it in the oven for about 1 hour, turning it a couple of times. While the pork is cooking halve the apricots and discard the stones. Mix together the amaretti crumbs, the icing-sugar and the egg with a fork until well combined: fill the apricot halves with the mixture. Line a baking-dish with parchment, put in the apricots and place them in the oven with the pork for about 10 minutes. Take the pork and the apricots out of the oven. Slice the pork, arrange it on a serving plate, surround it with the apricots and serve immediately, while it is very hot. You could substitute chicken, guinea fowl, duck or venison for the pork.

APRICOT AND RICE MOULD

300G/10OZ/2¼ CUPS RICE, ARBORIO IF
POSSIBLE
600ML/1PT/3¾ CUPS MILK
500G/1LB APRICOTS
3 LARGE EGG YOLKS
90G/3OZ/⅔ CUP ICING-SUGAR
240ML/8FL OZ/1 CUP DOUBLE
(HEAVY) CREAM

Bring a saucepan of water to the boil, put in the rice and cook for about 5 minutes. Drain, then pour the rice back into the saucepan, add the milk and cook, covered, over a very low heat for about 30 minutes, or until the milk has been completely absorbed. Leave it to cool. Put the apricots into a saucepan, reserving 6 for decoration, with a few tablespoons of water and cook them, covered, over a low heat for about 10 minutes until tender. Drain them, reserving 12, and purée the rest in a blender. Stir the apricot purée into the rice. Beat the egg yolks with the icing-sugar until creamy, then mix well into the rice. Beat the cream until it holds firm peaks and fold it into the rice mixture. Wet a 1-litre (2pt) mould and fill it with the rice mixture. Level the top and refrigerate it for at least 6 hours before turning it out on to a serving dish. Halve the remaining apricots and use to decorate. Serve either at room temperature or chilled.

PEACHES

(PRUNUS PERSICA)

'When, looking through his worship's garden gate,
Ripe peaches tempted, and you longed to eat.'
(JOHN DOBSON, ROBIN, A PASTORAL ELEGY, C 1740)

IT WOULD BE DIFFICULT for me to say which fruit is my favourite but peaches are definitely the one I most look forward to seeing again in the market with the return of summer. They are singularly sensual, fresh and sexy at the same time. A young woman's perfect complexion is compared to the velvety down and blush of a white peach. The plump curvaceous shape of the fruit has been likened to a voluptuous breast. The French have named a variety of peach Tetons de Venus, the breasts of Venus, and Renoir advised young artists to practise painting a peach before painting a nude woman. Few pleasures of the palate can be compared to biting into perfectly ripened peach flesh and feeling the juice run down your chin. Adam and Eve's downfall could just as easily have been caused by a peach as an apple.

Peaches were thought to have originated in Persia, thus their Latin name, ' the Persian plum'. Actually they came to Persia from China, their native land. Alexander the Great introduced them to ancient Greece and Rome. Today Italy produces about 80 per cent of the peaches consumed in Europe. I am told there are hundreds of varieties of peaches, but that has more to do with the kind of tree than differences in the fruit they produce. Once you have decided whether you want to buy white peaches, which some consider to have finer flavour, or yellow peaches, the problem is to select good ones.

I am happy to report that it is still possible to find a delicious peach at our local markets. It is, however, always something of a gamble, as the quality of peaches is very irregular, even among those in the same box. They do not ripen off the tree, so they should be firm, as they will soften in a day or two, or slightly soft, if you are going to eat them immediately. If you come away with a few hard peaches, you can always use them for cooking. If you have the misfortune of having chosen woolly ones, there is nothing to do but throw them on the compost heap.

The most simple way to enjoy a peach at the table is to slice the fruit and add it to a glass of white wine. A more sophisticated version of this delicious combination is the Bellini, the celebrated drink created by Giuseppe Cipriani, founder of Harry's Bar in Venice, made with one part juice from a white peach and three parts Prosecco. A more complicated recipe for peaches is the dessert created by the French chef, Auguste Escoffier for the Australian soprano, Nellie Melba, called Pêches Melba. The genius of this dish is the delicious combination of peaches and raspberries.

A very old Italian proverb says, 'Peel a fig for a friend and a peach for an enemy.' It would seem that even the ancients knew that most of the nutritional value of a peach is contained in its delicate, fuzzy skin.

PEACHES PANNA COTTA

15G/½OZ GELATINE LEAVES OR
CRYSTALS
480ML/16FL OZ/2 CUPS DOUBLE
(HEAVY) CREAM
120G/4OZ/½ CUP SUGAR
2 PEACHES, PEELED AND STONED

FOR THE DECORATION
1 PEACH, SLICED, OR 120G/4OZ
RASPBERRIES

Soften the gelatine leaves in cold water for about 5 minutes, then squeeze out the excess liquid. If using the gelatine crystals, dissolve them in a little water according to the packet instructions. Heat half of the cream in a saucepan with the sugar. Take the pan off the heat, put in the gelatine and stir until it has dissolved. Purée the peaches in the blender, then stir the pulp into the cream. Allow to cool. Whisk the rest of the cream until it forms soft peaks, then fold it into the peach mixture. Wet 6 individual moulds or ramekins, or a 1 litre (2-pt) mould, drain them, then fill them with the peach mixture. Put them in the refrigerator and leave them to set for at least 2 hours. (A large mould will take at least 4 hours to set.) To turn them out, slide the point of a knife around the edge of each panna cotta to loosen it, then invert the mould over a serving dish and shake. Decorate with the sliced peach or the raspberries.

CHOCOLATE PEACH TART

FOR THE PASTRY CASE
120G/4OZ/8 TBSP BUTTER
240G/8OZ/2 CUPS UNBLEACHED PLAIN
(ALL-PURPOSE) FLOUR
1 LARGE EGG
120G/4OZ/½ CUP SUGAR
120G/4OZ/1 CUP COCOA POWDER
2 TBSP PEACH JAM
2 PEACHES

FOR THE CHOCOLATE FILLING
90G/3OZ/6 TBSP BITTER CHOCOLATE
60G/2OZ/4 TBSP UNSALTED BUTTER
3 EGG YOLKS AND 2 EGG WHITES
90G/3OZ/6 TBSP SUGAR

Preheat the oven to 175°C/350°F/gas mark 4.

Put the butter, flour, egg, sugar and cocoa into a food processor and process until a dough has formed. Place it in a bowl and cover it with clingfilm, then leave it in the refrigerator for at least 1 hour but no more than 6. Now prepare the filling: melt the chocolate and the butter together in the top half of a double-boiler, or in a bowl over a pan of simmering water. Mix well and leave it to cool. Whisk the egg whites until they form soft peaks. Beat the egg yolks with the sugar until light and creamy, then gently stir in the chocolate. Fold in the egg whites. Butter and flour a 28-cm (11-inch) tart tin. Roll out the pastry dough and use it to line the tin. Spread the jam over the pastry base. Peel and stone the peaches, then quarter them and arrange them over the jam. Pour over the chocolate filling and bake for 40 minutes. Leave the tart to cool slightly in the tin, then turn it out on to a pretty plate and serve it either warm or cold.

NECTARINES

'The nectarine, and curious peach
Into my hands themselves to reach;'
(Andrew Marvell, The Garden, 1681)

The nectarine is of the same species as the peach, *Prunus persica.* Botanists have discovered that the only genetic difference between them is in a single gene, which makes peach skin fuzzy. Nectarines do not have it so their skin is smooth. Yet so closely related are they that nectarines will often grow on peach trees and sometimes a nectarine tree will produce some 'mutant' fuzzy fruit. In Italian nectarines are called pesca noce, a walnut-like peach, because without the fuzz they appear harder than a peach.

Nectarines can be used in the same way as peaches. The nectarines I find in the market have a slightly firmer flesh than most peaches and a taste that is somewhat richer and a little sharper. Without the fuzz to wipe off, some people prefer nectarines to peaches as a table and dessert fruit. Like peaches, white or yellow flesh nectarines are available.

NECTARINES WITH RASPBERRY SAUCE

6 NECTARINES, HALVED AND STONED
JUICE OF ½ LEMON
300G/10OZ FRESH RASPBERRIES
90G/3OZ/6 TBSP SUGAR
60ML/2FL OZ/¼ CUP RED WINE

Sprinkle the nectarines with the lemon juice to prevent them discolouring. Put the raspberries in a saucepan with the sugar and the wine and cook them over a low heat for about 20 minutes or until they are syrupy, when the cooking liquid coats the back of a spoon. Pass through a sieve then discard the seeds. Arrange the nectarines cut side up on a platter, pour over the raspberry sauce and refrigerate until they are needed. They are also excellent served warm.

NECTARINE CHAMPAGNE

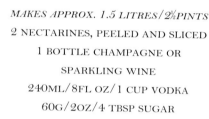

MAKES APPROX. 1.5 LITRES/2½PINTS
2 NECTARINES, PEELED AND SLICED
1 BOTTLE CHAMPAGNE OR
SPARKLING WINE
240ML/8FL OZ/1 CUP VODKA
60G/2OZ/4 TBSP SUGAR

Purée the nectarines in a blender. Take a carafe, pour into it the nectarine pulp, the champagne and the vodka. Stir in the sugar, add a few ice cubes and mix well. Serve immediately.

NECTARINE MERINGUE

6 NECTARINES, PEELED, HALVED AND
STONED
1 HANDFUL FRESH MINT LEAVES
90G/3OZ/6 TBSP CHOPPED HAZELNUTS
60ML/2FL OZ/¼ CUP DRY WHITE WINE
3 EGG WHITES, AT ROOM
TEMPERATURE
180G/6OZ/¾ CUP SUGAR

Preheat the oven to 175°C/350°F/gas mark 4.

Arrange the nectarines in an ovenproof dish and scatter over the mint leaves and hazelnuts, then pour over the wine. Put the dish in the oven and bake for 10 minutes. Take it out and leave it to cool. Increase the oven temperature to 200°C/400°F/gas mark 6.

Meanwhile, beat the egg whites until stiff peaks form. Still beating, add the sugar gradually until you have stiff peaks again. Spoon the meringue over the nectarines to cover them completely then bake for about 20 minutes until the surface is golden. Serve immediately, while still warm.

CHERRIES

(PRUNUS AVIUM / PRUNUS CERASUS)

'Cherry-ripe, ripe, ripe, I cry,
Full and fair ones; come and buy'

(HERRICK, CHERRY-RIPE 1648)

THE LOVELY BLOSSOMS of the almond tree are the first promise of spring in Italy. By early February they are already in full flower in Sicily. These are followed, after a seemingly endless pause, by the delicate and vulnerable apricot, evanescent as in a Chinese painting. When cherry-blossom time arrives, spring finally seems here to stay. The cherry is a generous tree and puts on a glorious show, producing profuse blossoms on boughs that will later be laden with abundant bunches of bright red fruit. Some types of cherry tree produce over a hundred pounds of fruit. The countryside around Vignola near Modena in the region of Emilia Romagna is the cherry capital of Italy. The Vignola cherry is deep red and deliciously sweet.

There are two distinct varieties of cherry, the sweet, prunus avium, and the sour, prunus cerasus. Sweet cherries grew wild in Asia Minor thousands of years ago, but it seems that the ancient Romans were the first to cultivate the sour type, still an Italian favourite. Cherries of both varieties come in a range of flavours as forceful as red wine grapes.

North American commercial growers prefer the Bing, probably because it is large and medium sweet, but we Italians prefer our sweet, more intensely flavoured Vignola. The most popular sour cherries in Italy are the Amarena and the Morello. The Morello has red flesh and a delicious red juice. It is sometimes called the Marasca and is soaked in alcohol and sweetened to make the liqueur, Maraschino. So-called Maraschino cherries are really Marascas preserved in Maraschino liqueur.

Once ripe, cherries mature all too quickly. They cannot be left on the tree for more than a week. Either they perish or the birds get to them first. The Latin name for sweet cherries means fruit 'of the birds'. Most commercial growers cover their trees with nets for protection. Unless you are small and nimble like my grandchildren, who love to climb into the branches of our local cherry tree to eat the fruit off the boughs and spit the seeds at each other, the only way to tell a well-ripened cherry and whether or not it is the sweet or sour kind is to taste it first from the market stall. (No self-respecting fruit vendor should begrudge you a few free cherries.) Colour is no help as both types come in all shades of red.

As a rule sweet cherries are for the table. Sour cherries are better in the kitchen, as their sharp flavour and firmer texture stands up to cooking. They make delicious preserves and sauces for meat, especially fowl. My grandchildren like to dip sweet cherries into chocolate, a venerable culinary combination.

CHERRY AND BARLEY SOUP

300G/10OZ PEARL BARLEY
2 BAY LEAVES
1.5 LITRES/2½PINTS/6 CUPS LIGHT
MEAT STOCK
500ML/16FL OZ/2 CUPS MILK
SALT
500G/1LB CHERRIES, STONED
90ML/3FL OZ/6 TBSP YOGURT

Put the barley into a bowl and cover it with water. Leave it to stand for about 12 hours, then drain it, put it into a deep saucepan with the bay leaves, stock, milk and a pinch of salt. Bring it to the boil, reduce the heat and cook, covered, for about 1 hour. Meanwhile, cook the cherries, covered, over a low heat with about 6 tablespoons of water for about 10 minutes. To serve, pour the soup into 6 deep bowls, discarding the bay leaves. Divide the cherries between them and finish each with a tablespoonful of yogurt. Serve immediately. Barley can be found in health-food shops.

SQUAB WITH CHERRIES

6 SQUAB OR WOOD PIGEON, CLEANED
6 BAY LEAVES
2 TBSP EXTRA-VIRGIN OLIVE OIL
60G/2OZ/2 TBSP UNSALTED BUTTER
60ML/2FL OZ/¼ CUP DRY WHITE WINE
6 SLICES COARSE COUNTRY BREAD
300G/10OZ CHERRIES, STONED
SALT AND PEPPER

Preheat the oven to 180°C/375°F/gas mark 5.

Put a bay leaf inside each squab, tie the legs closed with string and sprinkle with salt and pepper. Arrange the birds in a baking-dish with the oil and half of the butter. Roast them for 40 minutes, then turn them, pour in the wine and roast for another 20 minutes. Spread the bread with the rest of the butter and toast it until it is golden, about 5 minutes, then keep warm. Meanwhile, cook the cherries over a low heat with a few tablespoons of water for about 10 minutes. Drain and add the juice to the baking-dish with the squabs.

Place the toast on a serving dish, lay the squabs on it, then scatter over the cherries. Stir the cooking juices well, check the seasoning, then pour over the squabs.

DUCK BREASTS WITH CHERRY SAUCE

300G/10OZ CHERRIES, STONED
120ML/4FL OZ/½ CUP RED WINE
30G/1OZ/2 TBSP UNSALTED BUTTER
2 TBSP EXTRA-VIRGIN OLIVE OIL
6 DUCK BREASTS
SALT
3 TBSP VODKA

Put the cherries into a saucepan with the red wine and cook them, covered, over a low heat for about 20 minutes. Then purée them in a blender, and return them to the pan. Cook until the mixture is syrupy. Meanwhile, heat the butter and the oil in a frying-pan, put in the duck breasts and cook over a high heat for about 3 minutes on each side. Season with salt, pour over the vodka and continue to cook until the vodka has evaporated.

Arrange the duck breasts on a serving platter, cover them with the cherry sauce and serve immediately.

35

CRABAPPLE

(MALUS SYLVESTRIS)

IT CAME AS NEWS TO ME when I first read some years ago in an English publication that crabapples are too sour to eat: all my life I had nibbled at them happily on autumn walks through the Tuscan countryside. I like their sour, tangy bite.

Italians refer to crabapples simply as wild apples, *mela selvatica*. The English word, crab, sounds derogatory. It comes from the Scandinavian, meaning sour but in an unpleasant, bitter way, like a crabby person. There is nothing bitter about the wild apples I have tasted, although it is also true that most Italians seem to have a taste for acidic fruit. Maybe it balances the olive oil in our diet.

The crabapple is smaller than a regular apple and is brightly coloured, yellow and green with a red blush. Its only commercial use is in crabapple jelly. However, if your sweet tooth does not protest too much, you can use it in many of the recipes you would its cultivated cousins, apart from apple pie, of course.

CRABAPPLE WINE SAUCE

MAKES APPROX. 500ML / 1 PINT
12 CRABAPPLES, PEELED, CORED AND
SLICED
1 BOTTLE GOOD RED WINE
120G / 4OZ / ½ CUP SUGAR
1 PIECE CINNAMON STICK

Put the crabapples into a saucepan with
the wine, the sugar and the cinnamon.
Bring it to the boil, reduce the heat and
cook until it is syrupy, when it will coat
the back of a spoon or a drop on a plate
will remain perfectly round. Remove
and discard the cinnamon, then purée
the mixture in a blender and pour the
sauce into a bowl. Serve with boiled
ham, sautéed liver or roast pork. It also
makes an excellent accompaniment for
vanilla ice-cream.

CRABAPPLE SOUP

1 WHITE ONION, PEELED AND
CHOPPED
1 CELERY STALK, CHOPPED
60G/2OZ/4 TBSP UNSALTED BUTTER
30G/1OZ/2 TBSP PLAIN (ALL-PURPOSE)
FLOUR
2 TBSP CURRY POWDER
12 CRABAPPLES, PEELED, CORED AND
SLICED
150G/5OZ/6 TBSP RICE
1.5 LITRES/2½PT/6 CUPS MEAT STOCK
1 CHICKEN BREAST, SKINNED
240ML/8FL OZ/1 CUP DOUBLE
(HEAVY) CREAM
SALT

Put the onion and the celery in a saucepan with the butter and cook over a low heat for about 3 minutes or until the onion is translucent. Add the flour and stir for 1 minute. Add the curry powder, the crabapples, the rice, the stock and the chicken breast and bring them to the boil. Cook over a low heat, covered, for 30 minutes. Remove the chicken breast, dice it and set it aside. Then purée the rest of the soup mixture in a blender or pass it through a food mill. Return it to the saucepan, bring it back to the boil, then reduce the heat. Pour in the cream, add the diced chicken and cook for 5 minutes. Transfer the soup to a tureen and serve it very hot.

MEAT ROLL WITH CRABAPPLE

900G/2LB CHOPPED VEAL
90G/3OZ/6 TBSP FINE DRY
BREADCRUMBS
2 TBSP FLAT-LEAF PARSLEY, CHOPPED
1 TBSP GROUND BLACK PEPPER
2 LARGE EGGS
SALT
6 THIN RASHERS STREAKY BACON
PLAIN (ALL-PURPOSE) FLOUR FOR
DUSTING
60G/2OZ/4 TBSP UNSALTED BUTTER
2 TBSP EXTRA-VIRGIN OLIVE OIL
120ML/4FL OZ/½ CUP WHITE WINE
12 CRABAPPLES
3 TBSP WATER
6 TBSP CRANBERRY SAUCE
(See page 77)

Preheat the oven to 175°C/350°F/gas mark 4.

In a bowl, mix together the chopped veal, breadcrumbs, parsley, pepper and eggs, and season with salt. Shape the chopped veal into a rectangle and cover it with the bacon. Roll up the meat, with the bacon inside, to form a sausage shape, about 5cm (2in) in diameter. Dust the roll with the flour and put it in a baking-dish with 1 tablespoon of the butter and all of the oil. Roast for about 40 minutes. Turn the roll carefully, pour in the wine and cook for another 20 minutes.

Meanwhile, peel, core and halve the crabapples, then put them in a saucepan with the water and cook, covered, over a low heat for about 10 minutes until they are soft. Drain, then fill their cavities with the cranberry sauce. Slice the meat roll, lay it on a serving platter, surround it with the crabapples and serve immediately.

PLUMS

(PRUNUS DOMESTICA, SALICINA, AMERICANA)

'The blue was worn off, but the plum was well tasted.'

(MATTHEW PRIOR, JINNY THE JUST, C. 1708)

I CANNOT THINK OF a more splendid late-summer sight at the market than a basket of oval-shaped, smooth-skinned, bluish-black fruit with a beautiful bloom. These are our European plums (*prunus domestica*). They have a thick, sweet, yellow-green flesh that slips easily away from the stone, which also makes them ideal for drying.

There are over two thousand kinds of plum, differing in shape, colour, texture and taste, although only a few are found in shops. Many types are grown only for canning and drying. The more hardy Japanese plum (*prunus salicina*), originally from China, and native American varieties (*prunus americana*) are the most popular among commercial growers, even in Europe. One of the first to ripen is the Japanese Burbank, imported into America in the nineteenth century by Luther Burbank. It is a large purple-red fruit with golden flesh. The Satsuma, or blood plum, another common Japanese variety, is dark red with juicy, sweet red flesh. One American variety is called a Beach plum or in Italy a Maritime plum, because it thrives in sandy soil and grows near beaches. Another is the yellow Klamath or Sierra plum, a hardy type that likes the cool climate of higher elevations. Both tend to be sour and are best for preserves.

My preferred eating plum is the greengage, a European variety that was first cultivated in Italy by the Romans, then popularized in France during the Renaissance, where it was named the Reine Claude, after Queen Claude, the wife of François I, and in the eighteenth century brought to England by Sir William Gage. Gages are smallish, yellow-green fruit, with sweet, juicy golden flesh that has a honey flavour when fully ripened. They are marvellous eaten fresh and can be made into delicious jams and sauces.

A powerfully flavoured plum good for cooking is the damson, named after the ancient city of Damascus in Syria where they grew wild. They are small with blue skin and firm flesh that does not turn mushy when cooked. Their strong, almost spicy taste intensifies the flavour of meat dishes.

PLUM CHARLOTTE

180G/9OZ/1 CUP SUGAR
300ML/10FL OZ/1¼ CUPS WATER
JUICE OF 1 LEMON
600G/1¼LB PLUMS
15G/½OZ GELATINE LEAVES OR
CRYSTALS
4 EGG YOLKS
480ML/16FL OZ/2 CUPS DOUBLE
(HEAVY) CREAM
ABOUT 36 SPONGE FINGERS

Put half of the sugar into a saucepan with the water and the lemon juice. Bring it to the boil, then put in the plums and cook over a low heat for about 10 minutes. Drain, reserving the juices. Soften the gelatine leaves in cold water for about 10 minutes, then squeeze out the excess liquid. (If using gelatine crystals, dissolve them in a little water and proceed according to the packet instructions.) Reheat half of the plum juices over a low heat, add the gelatine and stir until it has dissolved. Beat the egg yolks with the rest of the sugar, then stir in half of the cream and all of the gelatine mixture. Pour into the top half of a double-boiler, or set the mixing bowl over a pan of simmering water, and cook over a medium heat, stirring continuously, without boiling, until it coats the back of a spoon. Let it cool completely. Beat the rest of the cream until it forms stiff peaks, then fold it into the cream mixture. Dip the sponge fingers into the rest of the plum juices and use them to line a 1.5-litre (3-pint) charlotte mould. Fill the mould with the plums, pour over the cream mixture, level the surface and refrigerate for at least 4 hours. When you are ready to serve, invert the mould over a plate to turn out. Serve either at room temperature or chilled.

PLUM CARAMEL SAUCE

MAKES ABOUT 300G/20FL OZ
600G/1¼LB PLUMS, BLANCHED,
PEELED, HALVED AND STONED
120G/4OZ/½ CUP SUGAR
2 TBSP KIRSCH

Put the plums into a saucepan, covered, over a low heat for about 10 minutes then purée them in the blender. In a small saucepan, cook the sugar until it has caramelized, turned brown, stirring from time to time. Take the pan off the heat and stir in the Kirsch carefully. Return the pan to the heat and stir in the plum purée until it is well combined. If the sauce seems too thick – this will depend on the quality of the plums – add a little water or a couple of tablespoonfuls of milk. Perfect with vanilla ice-cream or as an accompaniment to roast meat such as duck or pork.

CURRIED PLUM SAUCE

MAKES ABOUT 300G/20FL OZ
600G/1¼LB PLUMS, BLANCHED,
PEELED, HALVED AND STONED
1 APPLE, PEELED, CORED AND
QUARTERED
1 SMALL ONION, PEELED AND CHOPPED
SALT
1 TBSP CURRY POWDER
60G/2OZ/4 TBSP UNSALTED BUTTER

Put the plums, apple and onion into a saucepan and cook over a low heat for about 10 minutes or until they are soft. Add a little salt and the curry powder, mix well, then purée in a blender. Return the mixture to the saucepan and reheat it with the butter for a few minutes. Pour the sauce into a bowl and serve. Delicious with roast port, duck or boiled ham.

QUINCES

(PYRUS CYDONIA)

'Branches of quinces trained against
a wall make fine espaliers, and that concludes
all I have to say about this noble fruit.'

(GIACOMO CASTELVETRO,
THE FRUIT, HERBS AND VEGETABLES OF ITALY, 1614)

ONCE A FRIEND gave me a few quinces off his tree. Inadvertently I left them on the back seat of my car and forgot about them. A couple of days later the entire car was permeated by the most delicate and exquisite flowery scent. What amazed and pleased me was that it lasted for several weeks, even after I had removed the fruit. I should have remembered that until a relatively short time ago quinces were put in cupboards and chests to perfume household linens.

The quince has been cultivated for thousands of years. Originally it came from Persia and was esteemed by the ancient Greeks and Romans. Literary scholars identify it as the mythological 'golden apple' or 'apple of love', the fruit of Aphrodite. Medieval and Renaissance recipes frequently mention quince as a condiment for cooked meats, and in Venice, *mostarda veneta* is still prepared with quince seasoned with spices and hot mustard. It is an appetizing combination of sweet and hot tastes and is served as an accompaniment to boiled meats. Today quince rarely appears in Italian markets, perhaps because it must be cooked before it can be enjoyed. Quince off the tree is almost hard as a rock. When cooked or baked it softens to a perfect tenderness.

In Italy you are most likely to find quince preserved in the form of *cotognata*, quince cheese or butter. This is a speciality of the southern regions of the peninsula, particularly Puglia. It is made by very slowly reducing puréed quince in sugar. The resulting paste is spread on trays and left in the sun to dry. It turns a beautiful deep rose in colour and is so dense in texture it can be sliced into squares and served as a sweet. In shops it usually comes packed in little wooden boxes.

QUINCE JELLY ITALIAN STYLE

MAKES APPROXIMATELY 36 PIECES
2KG/4½LB QUINCES, WASHED AND
QUARTERED
60ML/2FL OZ/¼ CUP WATER
ABOUT 480G/16OZ/2 CUPS SUGAR
FEW DROPS ALMOND OIL

Put the quinces in a large saucepan with the water, cover, and cook over a low heat, stirring occasionally with a wooden spoon, for about 45 minutes, or until they are tender. Then pass them through a food mill or a sieve and discard the seeds and skin. Weigh the quince paste, then return it to the saucepan with the same weight of sugar, and cook over a low heat, uncovered, stirring from time to time, for about 40 minutes until it has thickened. Brush a baking-tin with the oil and spread the quince mixture about 2.5cm (1in) thick and level it with the back of a knife. Let it get cold, then cover it with a cloth and leave it to stand for about 2 weeks, perhaps in the sun, to become very firm. Cut it into rectangles 5cm (2in) x 2.5cm (1in) and store in an airtight tin. They will keep for at least 3 months. If you like, you can dust with sugar before you store them.

ROAST LAMB WITH QUINCES

1 LEG LAMB, ABOUT 2KG/4½LB
2 GARLIC CLOVES, PEELED AND
CHOPPED
2 SPRIGS THYME
SALT AND PEPPER
120G/4OZ/8 TBSP UNSALTED BUTTER
2 TBSP EXTRA-VIRGIN OLIVE OIL
4 QUINCES
JUICE OF 1 LEMON
1 TBSP SUGAR

Preheat the oven to 200°C/400°F/gas mark 6.

Make small cuts in the skin of the lamb and insert into them the garlic slices and the thyme leaves. Season the surface with salt and pepper. Put half of the butter and all of the oil in a roasting-tin, lay in the lamb and roast for about 45 minutes. The lamb should still be pink inside. Meanwhile, peel, core and dice the quinces. Sauté them in a frying-pan with the rest of the butter over a low heat for a few minutes, then add the lemon juice, a tablespoon of water, and continue to cook until tender, stirring occasionally, about 20 minutes. Stir in the sugar. To serve, carve the lamb, lay the slices on a platter and surround them with the diced quinces and their juices.

BAKED QUINCE

6 QUINCES, PEELED, CORED AND SEEDED

90G/3OZ/6 TBSP AMARETTI BISCUITS

90G/3OZ/6 TBSP RAISINS, STONED IF
NECESSARY

90G/3OZ/6 TBSP CHOPPED WALNUTS

GRATED ZEST AND JUICE OF 1 ORANGE

120G/4OZ/½ CUP SUGAR

6 TSP GRAND MARNIER

120ML/4FL OZ/½ CUP WATER

30G/1OZ/2 TBSP UNSALTED BUTTER

Preheat the oven to 175°C/350°F/gas mark 4.

With a spoon, make a cavity about 5cm (2in) in diameter in the centre of each quince. Crumble the amaretti and mix together with the raisins, walnuts, orange zest and juice, half of the sugar and the Grand Marnier, and use this to fill the cavities in the quinces. Arrange them in a deep baking-dish, pour in the water, scatter over the rest of the sugar, dot with the butter and cover with foil. Bake for about 1 hour, or until the quinces are tender, basting them occasionally with the cooking juices. Serve warm with thick cream.

MEDLARS

(MESPILUS GERMANICA)

'You'll be rotten ere you be half ripe,
and that's the right virtue of the medlar.'
(SHAKESPEARE, AS YOU LIKE IT, III, II)

TWO DIFFERENT TREES bearing very different fruit go by the name medlar. One, whose botanical name is *Mespilus germanica*, and in Italian is known as *nespola commune*, is a native of Europe. I must confess I have never seen either the tree or its fruit. I am told it is about the size of a small apricot, reddish-brown in colour, of an odd shape with a distinctive open end. Jane Grigson in her ever informative Fruit Book, says the old English name for the medlar was openarse and that the provincial French in the last century called it cul de chien. All of which makes me feel I don't really need to see one. In ancient times it was valued for its medicinal quality, but contemporary culinary writers who know the fruit advise not to bother with it in the kitchen. It is so hard when ripe that it cannot be eaten until rotten. So if you have never tasted a medlar either, it seems we have not missed much. Altogether it sounds a most unpleasant fruit.

On the other hand the second species, called the loquat or Japanese medlar (*Eriobotrya japonica*), bears a lovely little apricot-coloured fruit that grows in clusters on the branch. The loquat tree is a handsome evergreen that grows wild in most temperate climates and provides welcome shade. You see them thriving in the urban sprawl on the outskirts of Naples. In Tuscany they are often planted as an ornamental addition to back gardens. In the southern Mediterranean they are also commercially grown, although in diminishing quantities. It always surprises visitors, from countries who disdain this humble fruit, to see them on sale in our markets.

The loquat fruit has white or yellow flesh and the flavour of an orangy pear, with a sweet-sour taste, that gets sweeter the further south it is grown. Inside it has five large stones, which do not leave much room for flesh, so when buying loquats to cook you will need to take that into consideration.

MEDLARS WITH SAUTEED CHICKEN LIVERS

30G/1OZ/2 TBSP UNSALTED BUTTER
2 TBSP EXTRA-VIRGIN OLIVE OIL
600G/1¼LB CHICKEN LIVERS
SALT AND PEPPER
2 TBSP WHITE WINE VINEGAR
480G/1LB MEDLARS, PEELED, HALVED
AND STONED

Heat the butter and the oil in a frying-pan, put in the chicken livers and sauté them for a few minutes over a high heat – if the heat is too low they will dry out and toughen – turning them occasionally. Season, add the vinegar and cook until it has evaporated. Put in the medlars, then sauté, covered, shaking the pan, for a couple more minutes. Serve immediately. The slight pungency of the medlars complements the chicken livers well.

MEDLAR ICE-CREAM

600G/1¼LB MEDLARS, PEELED AND
STONED
4 LARGE EGG YOLKS
120G/4OZ/½ CUP SUGAR
480ML/16FL OZ/2 CUPS MILK
4 TBSP HONEY
240ML/8FL OZ/1 CUP DOUBLE
(HEAVY) CREAM

Purée the medlars in a blender. Beat the egg yolks with the sugar until light and fluffy, then add the milk a little at a time. Pour the mixture into the upper half of a double-boiler, or set the mixing bowl over a pan of simmering water, then cook, stirring continuously, over a medium heat until it starts to thicken and coats the back of the spoon. Don't let it boil. Take the pan off the heat and stir in the puréed medlars and the honey. Allow to cool. Beat the cream stiffly and fold it into the medlar mixture. Pour it into an ice-cream machine and freeze according to the manufacturer's instructions. If you do not have a machine, pour the mixture into a suitable bowl and put it into the freezer for at least 4 hours. After the first 30 minutes, take it out and whisk to break up the ice crystals then return it to the freezer. Whisk twice more at half-hourly intervals, then return it to the freezer and allow it to set firm.

Medlar ice-cream is delicious with pears cooked in a little white wine.

MEDLAR FRUIT SALAD WITH LEMON AND MINT

600G/1¼LB MEDLARS, WASHED,
HALVED AND STONED
JUICE AND ZEST OF 1 LEMON
3 TBSP SUGAR
1 HANDFUL FRESH MINT LEAVES

Put the medlars in a bowl, sprinkle them with the lemon juice and zest, and the sugar. Stir gently, then cover with the mint leaves and serve.

If preferred, you can peel the medlars, but as the skin is not tough this is not really necessary.

SOFT FRUIT

STRAWBERRIES

(FRAGARIA)

'Doubtless God could have made a better berry,
but doubtless God never did.'
(ISAAK WALTON, THE COMPLEAT ANGLER, C. 1633)

ONE WINTRY LATE JANUARY MORNING of this year I made my way down the snowy road from Coltibuono, our family home in Tuscany, to the little town of Gaiole in Chianti at the bottom of the hill to do some shopping. There at the greengrocery, with snow on the doorstep, I saw several boxes of large strawberries, looking like perfectly preserved fossils from last summer. They had come from Israel and I was assured they were delicious but I wasn't tempted – 'For everything there is a season.' In a few months my own June-bearer strawberry plants would be producing their fragrant fruit.

The strawberry is a member of the rose family and its cultivation has a long history in southern Europe. Ancient Greeks and Romans were fond of them and in medieval and Renaissance times they were much appreciated for their therapeutic properties. In the seventeenth century, Castelvetro recommended a concoction of strawberry roots and leaves as a mouthwash, that 'hardens the gums, strengthens the teeth and clears catarrh'.

Two types of 'wild' strawberries were cultivated then as well as now, the wood strawberry (*Fragaria vesca*) and the mountain or alpine strawberry (*Fragaria montana*). These are small and aromatic and produce a burst of bright berry taste,

a little sour early in the season and intensely sweet in the summer.

Today's larger, garden strawberry originally came from North America in the eighteenth century. It is a cross between two native species, the Virginia or scarlet strawberry and the Chilean or beach strawberry. Because of its distinct fragrance and flavour a common variety is called the pineapple strawberry. And, like the pineapple, the strawberry is botanically an 'aggregate fruit'. Each of its little black dots is a true fruit.

Offhand I can't think of any fruit plant easier to grow and enjoy in your garden than the strawberry. They are perennials that are ornamental as well as practical. They produce attractive green leaves, pretty white flowers and, of course, provide the immense pleasure of picking and eating a sun-ripened fruit straight from the vine.

When I buy strawberries I let my nose be my guide. Aroma rather than colour is the best indication of quality. I tend to choose the smaller ones as the large specimens that green grocers like to show off are often tasteless. If you have to clean strawberries it is best to wipe them with a damp cloth, like mushrooms, rather than wash them.

STRAWBERRY TIRAMISU

300G/10OZ MASCARPONE
180G/6OZ SPONGE FINGERS
240ML/8FL OZ/1 CUP SWEET WHITE
WINE – VIN SANTO, SAUTERNE OR
SIMILAR
300G/10OZ STRAWBERRIES,
PREFERABLY WILD, HULLED
240ML/8FL OZ/1 CUP DOUBLE
(HEAVY) CREAM

Spread half of the mascarpone on the
bottom of a serving bowl. Lay the
sponge fingers on a plate, pour over the
wine and leave them to absorb it. Then
arrange them over the mascarpone and
cover with half the strawberries. Spread
the rest of the mascarpone on top and
level it with a knife. Whip the cream to
stiff peaks, then put it into an icing-bag
with a fluted nozzle and squeeze it over
the mascarpone. Chill for at least 2
hours. Just before serving, scatter over
the remaining strawberries. To make
individual puddings, you can use trifle
sponges. Cut 6 sponge circles, soak in
the wine and assemble the tiramisu as
above, dividing the ingredients equally.

STRAWBERRY AND RICOTTA ROLL

210G/7OZ STRAWBERRIES, HULLED

480ML/16FL OZ/2 CUPS DRY WHITE
WINE

300G/10OZ RICOTTA

2 LARGE EGG YOLKS

90G/3OZ/6 TBSP SUGAR

300G/10OZ PUFF PASTRY, FRESHLY
MADE OR DEFROSTED

Preheat the oven to 175°C/350°F/gas mark 4.

Cut the strawberries in half vertically and put them into a bowl. Cover them with the wine and leave them to stand for about 2 hours, then drain. Whisk the ricotta with the egg yolks and the sugar until creamy and well blended. Roll the pastry into a rectangle measuring 30cm (10in) by 20cm (7in). Spread over the ricotta mixture and cover it with the strawberries. Roll up the pastry as you would a swiss roll, to form a cylinder, place it on a buttered baking sheet and bake for 40 minutes, or until it is golden and crisp on top. Serve either warm or cold.

CARAMELIZED STRAWBERRIES WITH LEMON CREAM

FOR THE LEMON CREAM

480ML/16FL OZ/2 CUPS MILK

120G/4OZ/½ CUP SUGAR

30G/1OZ/2 TBSP PLAIN (ALL-PURPOSE)
FLOUR

6 EGG YOLKS

GRATED ZEST OF 2 LEMONS

FOR THE STRAWBERRIES

300G/10OZ LARGE FRESH
STRAWBERRIES

210G/7OZ/1 CUP SUGAR

2 TBSP WATER

1 TBSP ALMOND OIL

First make the lemon cream. Scald the milk, then put the sugar and flour into a bowl and mix them well. Beat in the egg yolks with a wooden spoon until they are well blended. Now stir in the milk, a little at a time, then the lemon zest. Transfer the mixture to the top half of a double-boiler, or set the mixing bowl over a pan of simmering water, and cook, stirring continuously, over a medium heat, until the custard begins to boil. Pour it into a shallow serving dish and chill.

Clean the strawberries but don't remove the stems and leaves. Put the sugar into a heavy-bottomed saucepan with the water and cook over a low heat until it has caramelized and turned golden. Brush a flat surface with the oil. Take the saucepan off the heat and, holding them by the stems, dip the strawberries into the caramel one at a time, then lay them to cool on the oiled surface. (If the strawberries have no stems, spear them on a cocktail stick and dip them into the caramel.) When they are cold, arrange them on the lemon cream and serve immediately: if they sit on the cream for long the caramel will dissolve.

RASPBERRIES

(RUBUS IDAEUS VULGATUS)

'*All raspberries are good, some few are better.*'
(BUNYARD, THE EPICURE'S COMPANION, 1937)

IF I HAD TO CHOOSE a 'desert island' berry, it would be, without hesitation, the raspberry. Unfortunately for me it is not cultivated in the Mediterranean, although it grows in the higher elevations of Piemonte and Lombardia. Raspberries prefer a cooler climate. I hear that tiny, wonderfully fragrant ones thrive in Alaska. My idea of raspberry heaven are those fields I have seen in Herefordshire, England, where anyone can pick their own, as many as they want, and for a bargain price as well. I have eaten tasty wild raspberries in the Italian Tyrol, the Alpine area between Italy and Austria, but cultivated ones are wonderfully delicious too.

There are two species of the red raspberry, the European and the American (Rubus *idaeus trigosus*), as well as the black raspberry (Rubus *idaeus occidentalis*). Our native European raspberries are long and conical, while the American ones are round. Both types produce a yellow mutation that rarely makes it to market, because it is so soft. People say the best raspberries in Europe grow in Scotland and the finest in America are found in the Pacific Northwest, Oregon and Washington.

Off the cane, the raspberry is a delicate fruit. It is composed of numerous individual drupelets, held together by very fine hairs. When picked its stem and base stay on the plant leaving it hollow. Watch out when you buy them that those at the bottom of the basket aren't all crushed. Raspberries make delicious jam and sauce but don't kill their slightly acidic flavour with too much sugar.

A bowl of fresh raspberries straight from the cane resembles nothing so much as a bowl of jewels. Their sharp-sweet so-delicious taste is best enjoyed just as it is. Those with a sweeter tooth than mine might want to add a little fresh cream and sugar. In Italy raspberries are sometimes macerated in good red wine, and raspberries and fresh peaches are an ambrosial combination.

I remember a few years back when raspberry vinegar was all the range in Britain and America but I never understood why. On the other hand, in the Alsace region of France they make a spirit from wild raspberries called *framboise sauvage*, which is definitely worth a detour.

RASPBERRIES WITH BAKED MERINGUE

6 LARGE EGGS, SEPARATED
240G/8OZ/2 CUPS ICING-SUGAR
1LTR/1¾ PT/4 CUPS MILK
240G/8OZ/1 CUP SUGAR
30G/1OZ/2 TBSP PLAIN (ALL-PURPOSE)
FLOUR
300G/10OZ RASPBERRIES

Preheat the grill.

Whisk the egg whites with the icing-sugar until they form a stiff meringue. Bring the milk to a simmer in a large saucepan. Wet a serving spoon with cold water and use it to scoop up a spoonful of the meringue mixture. Slide it into the simmering milk and repeat with the rest of the mixture. Cook the meringues for a couple of minutes on one side then gently turn them over and cook for another minute. Remove them from the milk with a slotted spoon and leave them to drain and cool, spaced apart on a damp surface. Pass the milk through a sieve and measure off about 500ml (1pt). Beat the egg yolks with the sugar until fluffy, then stir in the flour and the reserved milk. Pour the mixture into the top half of a double-boiler, or set the mixing bowl over a pan of simmering water, and cook until the custard has thickened. Pour it into a large ovenproof dish and cover it with the raspberries. Dot the meringues over the top and put the dish under the grill until the meringue begins to colour. Serve immediately, very hot.

CHOCOLATE RAVIOLI WITH RASPBERRY SAUCE

210G/7OZ/1⅛ CUPS PLAIN
(ALL-PURPOSE) FLOUR
90G/3OZ/6 TBSP COCOA
3 LARGE EGGS
600G/1¼LB RASPBERRIES
120G/4OZ/½ CUP SUGAR
240G/8OZ RICOTTA

Put the flour and the cocoa into a mixing bowl and make a well in the centre. Break in the eggs and work them in with a fork, in a circular motion, until well combined. Put the dough on a work surface and knead until it is soft and smooth. Cover it with clingfilm and leave it to rest until the filling is ready.

Put the raspberries and the sugar into a saucepan and cook over a low heat, covered, until the juice has evaporated. Stir a third of the raspberries into the ricotta and purée the rest in the blender. Sieve the raspberry pulp and discard the seeds. Put the sauce into a bowl and set it aside.

Roll out the dough paper thin and cut it into 5-cm (2in) squares. Lay out half of the squares on a work surface, then put a scant teaspoon of the ricotta mixture on to each piece. Cover them with the rest of the dough squares and press them together to seal in the filling. Bring a saucepan of water to the boil, drop in the ravioli, a few at a time, and cook until they float to the surface. Drain and rinse them quickly under cold running water, which will prevent them sticking together. Repeat until all the ravioli are cooked. Serve with the raspberry sauce, handed round separately. The ravioli and the sauce can be served hot, if you prefer, as soon as the ravioli are done: you will need to cook them all together so that you can serve them before they cool and stick to each other.

RASPBERRY BREAD

30G/1OZ/2 TBSP FRESH YEAST
210ML/7FL OZ/¾ CUP LUKEWARM
WATER
360G/12OZ/3 CUPS PLAIN (ALL-
PURPOSE) FLOUR, PLUS A LITTLE
EXTRA FOR DUSTING
90G/3OZ/6 TBSP SUGAR
240G/8OZ RASPBERRIES

In a small bowl combine the yeast with the water and leave it to dissolve, about 10 minutes. Then, in a large bowl, mix together the flour with the sugar and the yeast water, working with a fork, in a circular motion, until all the liquid has been absorbed. Knead the dough briefly on a work surface until it is smooth, then gently work in the raspberries. Put the dough into a bowl dusted with flour and cover it tightly with clingfilm. Leave it to rise for about an hour, or until it has doubled in size. Divide the dough into 2 and shape it into long loaves about 5 cm (2in) in diameter. Lay them in a roasting-tin, or similar and leave them to rise again for about 20 minutes. Meanwhile preheat the oven to 200°C/400°F gas mark 6. Bake the raspberry bread for 30 minutes, or until the bottom of the loaf sounds hollow when tapped. Leave the bread to cool before serving.

MULBERRIES

(MORUS NIGRA)

*'Now I come to that really useful tree, the mulberry,
which we treasure both for its leaves, on which the noble
silkworm feeds, and its delicious fruit,'*
(GIACOMO CASTELVETRO,
THE FRUIT, HERBS AND VEGETABLES OF ITALY, 1614)

THE MULBERRY IS A marvellous tree, which grows tall and broad. Like the fig, to which it is related, it will take root anywhere and everywhere. Very ancient ones can be found in Italy, dating from the time when there was a flourishing Italian silk industry. The tree cultivated for the silkworm is called a 'white mulberry' because it produces a white berry. Centuries ago, someone discovered that the worms that ate the leaves of the white mulberry (morus alba) produced the best silk. Castelvetro, the seventeenth-century writer on Italian fruit, notes that white mulberries were also excellent for fattening chickens and other fowl. Humans, especially children, prefer to eat the berries from the 'black mulberry', which look much like blackberries except they are long and oval and have a sharper flavour.

Like all mothers I have always had an ambiguous admiration for mulberries. The tree is an asset to any garden but the juice of the berry indelibly stains everything it touches.

As far as I know there are no commercial plantings of black mulberry trees. The fruit is difficult to market because it perishes within a day or two of picking.

For all culinary purposes the mulberry is interchangeable with the common blackberry. As a matter of fact, when reading through old Italian recipes it is not clear whether they call for blackberries or mulberries, since the name of the fruit is the same, *mora*. Anyhow, it does not make any significant difference. Maestro Martini, the fifteenth-century chef and cookery writer, gives a recipe in his book *Libro de Arte Coquinaria* for *sapor di moroni*, a sauce consisting of pounded almonds, breadcrumbs, and moroni, seasoned with cinnamon, ginger and nutmeg, which would work very well with either fruit.

SQUID WITH MULBERRIES

600G/1¼LB SQUID, CLEANED
120G/4OZ STALE BREAD
210G/7OZ MULBERRIES, HULLED
1 LARGE EGG
SALT AND PEPPER
1 TBSP EXTRA-VIRGIN OLIVE OIL
120ML/4FL OZ/½ CUP DRY WHITE
WINE

Cut the tentacles off the squid and chop them. Soak the bread in some water for 5 minutes, squeeze it dry then mix it with the tentacles and the mulberries. Stir in the egg to bind the mixture and season with salt and pepper. Fill the cuttlefish cavities with this stuffing and secure the open end with cocktail sticks. Heat the oil in a frying-pan and sauté the squid for about 10 minutes over a medium heat, until they turn golden. Then pour in half of the wine, cover the pan, lower the heat and cook for about 1 hour, adding the rest of the wine as needed to keep the squid moist. To serve, arrange the squid on a large platter with the juices poured around and eat while it is hot.

MULBERRY AND MASCARPONE CUPS

300G/10OZ MULBERRIES, HULLED
180G/6OZ/⅜ CUP SUGAR
2 LARGE EGG YOLKS
3 TBSP RUM
300G/10OZ MASCARPONE CHEESE

Put the mulberries into a saucepan with half of the sugar and cook over a low heat for about 10 minutes. Drain off the mulberries, set them aside, and continue to cook the juice until it is syrupy – a drop poured on to a plate will stay perfectly round. Return the mulberries to the pan, stir and set aside. Whisk the rest of the sugar with the egg yolks until creamy, then stir in the rum and the mascarpone. Pour the mulberries into a serving bowl, cover them with the mascarpone mixture and refrigerate until you are ready to serve.

CREPES WITH MULBERRY SAUCE

300G/10OZ MULBERRIES
120G/4OZ/½ CUP SUGAR
4 TBSP WATER

FOR THE CREPES (MAKES 12):
120G/4OZ/1 CUP PLAIN
(ALL-PURPOSE) FLOUR
PINCH SALT
1 LARGE EGG PLUS 1 LARGE EGG YOLK
300ML/½ PINT/1¼ CUPS MILK
1 TBSP MELTED BUTTER
OIL FOR FRYING

Purée the berries in a food processor. If preferred you can remove the seeds by pressing the purée through a sieve but I prefer to keep them in. Boil the sugar and water in a saucepan until syrupy (a drop on a flat surface should stay round). Allow to cool and then add to the mulberries. Set aside while you make the crêpes.

Sift the flour and salt into a mixing bowl and make a well in the centre. Crack the egg and yolk into the centre and add half the milk. Stir from the middle, drawing in the flour from the sides of the bowl. Stir in the remaining milk and melted butter. If there are any lumps, strain the batter through a sieve. Heat a 15cm (6in) omelette or crêpe pan and oil lightly. Pour about 2 tbsp batter into the centre and lift and tilt the pan so the batter spreads. Turn to cook the second side and repeat until the batter is all used up.

Serve the crêpes with ice-cream and the warm mulberry sauce.

BLACKBERRIES

(RUBUS FRUCTICOSUS)

'If reasons were as plentiful as blackberries...'
(SHAKESPEARE, HENRY IV, PART 1, II, IV)

BLACKBERRIES ARE CLOSELY RELATED to raspberries and almost as good – some would say even better. For me they have the advantage of growing wild all over our woods in September and October. Blackberry bramble is part of the classical macchia mediterranea, or Mediterranean scrub. Picking wild blackberries in the woods has been such a popular tradition for so many centuries that there exists an Italian expression, *andare per more*, which translates as 'to go blackberrying'.

Reddish-black, shiny blackberries, like their raspberry cousin, are an aggregate fruit composed of individual drupelets. Their canes, however, are thornier, which makes picking them something of a challenge. A larger, juicier, thornless blackberry has been developed for commercial plantings. As one might suspect, in keeping with the folk wisdom of no rose without a thorn, blackberries with thorns are said to have the best flavour. Because they can tolerate more sun and heat, blackberries are also more prolific and sweeter than raspberries, although the little seeds in each drupelet of the wild blackberry are harder.

In Italy fresh blackberries, with wild strawberries, raspberries, blueberries and redcurrants, comprise what is called *sottobosco*, 'wild berries from the woods'. In late summer and early autumn you will see little wooden boxes of this mixture displayed in market shops and in good restaurants. The fruit is eaten as it is, or with lemon and sugar. Often a sauce is made from *sottobosco* to go with *pannacotta*, moulded cooked cream served cold.

It is worth remembering that both raspberries and blackberries freeze well. Lay them out in a single layer on a baking sheet first, then when they are solid pack them into a suitable container.

BLACKBERRY JAM

MAKES APPROXIMATELY 500G/1LB
1KG/2¼LB BLACKBERRIES
240G/8OZ/1 CUP SUGAR
PEEL OF 4 APPLES
PEEL OF 1 LEMON

Put the blackberries, the sugar, the apple and lemon peel into a large saucepan and cook over a low heat, covered, stirring occasionally, for about 10 minutes. Discard the peel, then sieve the pulp and discard the seeds. If you prefer to keep the seeds in, simply continue cooking over a low heat for another hour, or until it is syrupy, when a drop poured on to a plate remains perfectly round. Pour immediately into a clean, sterilized, warmed glass jar and seal it tightly. It will keep in a cool, dark place for up to 3 months, but no longer as the sugar content is low. When you have opened it, keep it in the refrigerator and use it within 1 week.

BLACKBERRY TORTE

2 LARGE EGGS
120G/4OZ/1 CUP PLAIN (ALL-PURPOSE)
FLOUR, PLUS 3 TBSP FOR DUSTING
120G/4OZ/½ CUP SUGAR
2 TBSP BAKING POWDER
120G/4OZ/8 TBSP MELTED BUTTER,
PLUS EXTRA FOR GREASING THE TIN
600G/1¼LB BLACKBERRIES

Preheat the oven to 175°C/350°F/gas mark 4.

In a large bowl, beat the eggs with a fork. Then, a little at a time, beat in the flour, the sugar and the baking powder. Stir in the butter, then fold in the blackberries. Butter and flour a 23-cm (9in) springform cake tin. Pour in the batter and bake for about 1 hour. After the first 40 minutes, take out the cake, cover the top with foil and return it to the oven for the last 20 minutes. When you take it out again, remove the foil and leave the torte to cool slightly in the tin. Then open the springform and turn it out on to a serving plate. Eat either warm or at room temperature.

BLACKBERRY PANNA COTTA

15G/½OZ GELATINE LEAVES OR
CRYSTALS
120G/4OZ/½ CUP SUGAR
480ML/1PT/2 CUPS DOUBLE
(HEAVY) CREAM
480G/1LB BLACKBERRIES

Put the gelatine leaves into a bowl, cover them with cold water and leave them to soften for about 10 minutes. Drain, and squeeze out the excess liquid. If using gelatine crystals, dissolve following the instructions on the packet.

Meanwhile, put the sugar and half of the cream into a saucepan and heat it gently, but do not let it boil. Turn off the heat, add the gelatine and stir until it has dissolved. Leave it to cool. Beat the rest of the cream until it forms stiff peaks. Purée the blackberries in a food processor with plastic blades, then sieve the pulp and discard the seeds. Stir the blackberry purée into the gelatine mixture, then fold in the whipped cream. Wet a 1-litre (2pt) bowl and fill it with the blackberry cream mixture, then leave it in the refrigerator to set for at least 4 hours. To turn it out, slide a knife around the edge of the bowl to loosen the panna cotta, then invert it over a serving dish and shake.

BLUEBERRIES

(VACCINIUM SPECIES)

'As American as blueberry pie!'
(A SAYING)

FOR SEVERAL YEARS my youngest son went to summer camp in New England and returned with an appetite for blueberries – blueberry pie, blueberry muffins, blueberry pancakes, blueberry cheesecake – that I was unable to satisfy at home. I insisted that our *mirtilli* were blueberries, and I was also sure they had to be just as good if not better than the American kind. He disagreed.

As it turned out, he was right and I was wrong. European *mirtilli, vaccinium myrtillus*, are bilberries, in French *myrtille*. The berries, however, are related, two species of the genus *vaccinium*. Both grow wild on a shrublike bush, single blue-black berries in a little bunch of three or four, but the American blueberry, especially the cultivated kind, *vaccinium corymbosum*, is larger and sweeter. The bilberry has a slightly acidic flavour.

The blueberry is also closely related to the huckleberry, which is smaller and darker with a tougher skin and seeds inside. It tastes more like the bilberry, which is also called the whortleberry or blaeberry. Blueberries and bilberries can be used in exactly the same way. When cooked I think you would have to be a connoisseur, like my son, to tell the difference.

RICOTTA AND BLUEBERRY MOULDS

600G/1¼LB RICOTTA
120G/4OZ/½ CUP SUGAR
600G/1¼LB/3 CUPS BLUEBERRIES
1 HANDFUL FRESH MINT LEAVES

In a bowl, whisk the ricotta with half of the sugar until it is well blended. Divide the ricotta mixture between 6 individual ramekins. Press the surface lightly to expel any air bubbles, then chill in the refrigerator until you are ready to serve.

Meanwhile, put the blueberries into a saucepan with the rest of the sugar and the mint, and cook over a low heat for about 10 minutes. Drain the blueberries, reserving the juices, discard the mint, then reduce the liquid until is syrupy – a drop poured on to a plate will stay perfectly round. Return the blueberries to the juices in the pan and reheat them for about 2 minutes. Meanwhile, turn out the moulds: slip the point of a knife around the edges, then invert each one over a dessert bowl. Pour the warmed blueberries around the ricotta and serve immediately.

BLUEBERRY AND YOGURT ICE-CREAM

900G/1LB 14OZ/4½ CUPS BLUEBERRIES
750ML/1¼PT/3 CUPS YOGURT
90G/3OZ/6 TBSP SUGAR

Reserve a third of the blueberries for decoration and purée the rest in a blender. Pour in the yogurt and the sugar and blend again until they are thoroughly combined. Tip the mixture into an ice-cream machine and follow the manufacturer's instructions. If you do not have a machine, pour the mixture into a suitable container and put it into the freezer for at least 4 hours. After the first 30 minutes, take it out and whisk it to break up the ice crystals, then return it to the freezer. Whisk twice more at half-hourly intervals, then leave the ice-cream to become firm. To serve, scoop the ice-cream into dessert bowls and scatter over the remaining blueberries.

BLUEBERRY GRAPPA

300G/10OZ/1¾ CUPS BLUEBERRIES,
WASHED AND DRIED
1 BOTTLE GRAPPA

You will need either a large jar with an efficient seal or cork – perhaps a Kilner jar – or a large bottle that will hold the blueberries and the grappa, also with a tight cap or a cork

Put the blueberries into the jar or bottle and pour over the grappa. Seal, and leave it in a cool, dark place for at least 3 months before drinking, turning it occasionally.

CRANBERRIES

(OXYCOCCUS PALUSTRIS)

'The dinner ending with a good tart of cranberries.'
(QUEEN VICTORIA, A LIFE IN THE HIGHLANDS, 1868)

I TASTED MY FIRST CRANBERRIES in the form of sauce at a Thanksgiving dinner given by American neighbours in Tuscany. They used to send home for cranberries for their holiday turkey. Now you can find bottled cranberry sauce in any supermarket.

The Native Americans of New England valued the cranberry because it kept fresh all winter due to its waxy skin. Some of the English colonists would have known it from their homeland but they must have been pleasantly surprised, given their meagre circumstances, to find that the North American variety, *Oxycoccus macrocarpus*, was bigger and better. Several centuries later their descendants are cultivating cranberries on an industrial scale and exporting them back to Britain and other countries, frozen, canned, dried and in sauces and jellies. Because cranberries are especially high in iron and potassium, cranberry juice is now much recommended in the daily diet of the elderly.

I love the cranberry's distinctively tart taste and the sharp flavour it adds to other dishes. If freshly frozen ones were more easily found in Italy, I would certainly use them more frequently. Recently I read that when a British cookery expert mentioned cranberries favourably on her TV programme, she set off such a cranberry craze that afterwards not a cranberry could be found throughout the entire British Isles – which would have pleased the descendants of the Pilgrim Fathers.

CRANBERRY SOUP

600G/1¼LB/3 CUPS CRANBERRIES
3 TBSP CORNFLOUR
500ML/16FL OZ/2 CUPS WATER
500ML/16FL OZ/2 CUPS RED WINE
1 TBSP SUGAR
GRATED ZEST OF 1 ORANGE
3 TBSP UNSALTED BUTTER
6 SLICES COARSE COUNTRY BREAD

Put the cranberries into a saucepan, sprinkle over the cornflour and cook over a low heat for a couple of minutes, stirring with a wooden spoon. Pour in the water and the wine, add the sugar and the orange zest, then continue to cook for 30 minutes. Heat the butter in a large frying-pan, put in the bread and cook for about 5 minutes on each side until golden. Place a slice of bread in each serving bowl, pour over the cranberry soup and serve immediately, very hot.

VEAL WITH CRANBERRIES

300G/10OZ/1½ CUPS CRANBERRIES
1 TBSP MUSTARD POWDER
60G/2OZ/4 TBSP SUGAR
600G/1¼LB MILK-FED VEAL ESCALOPES,
THINLY SLICED
2 TBSP EXTRA-VIRGIN OLIVE OIL
30G/1OZ/2 TBSP UNSALTED BUTTER
120ML/4FL OZ/½ CUP DRY WHITE
WINE
60ML/2FL OZ/¼ CUP DOUBLE
(HEAVY) CREAM
SALT

Put the cranberries into a saucepan with the mustard, the sugar and a little water, then cook them for about 10 minutes over a low heat or until the liquid has almost evaporated. Leave to cool completely. Spread the sliced veal over a work surface and divide the cranberries between them. Roll up the veal slices, with the cranberries inside, and secure them with a cocktail stick. Heat the oil and the butter in a frying-pan, put in the veal rolls and sauté them over a medium heat, turning them occasionally, for about 10 minutes. Pour in the wine and the cream, season with salt, and continue to cook until the sauce has thickened a little. Serve hot with a little of the cranberry sauce from the following recipe, if desired.

BOLLITO MISTO WITH CRANBERRY SAUCE

3L/6PT WATER
300G/10OZ BEEF, SUITABLE FOR
BOILING
1 CARROT, PEELED AND ROUGHLY
CHOPPED
1 CELERY STALK, ROUGHLY CHOPPED
1 ONION, PEELED AND ROUGHLY
CHOPPED
1 HANDFUL FLAT-LEAF PARSLEY
1 FRESH BAY LEAF
SALT
300G/10OZ VEAL, SUITABLE FOR
BOILING
ABOUT 600G/1¼LB CHICKEN
300G/10OZ BOILING SAUSAGE, E.G.
COTECHINO
300G/10OZ CRANBERRIES
150G/5OZ/⅔ CUP SUGAR

Bring the water to the boil in a large saucepan, then reduce the heat to a simmer, put in the beef, the vegetables, herbs and a little salt, then cook for about 1 hour. Add the veal and the chicken and continue to cook for another hour. Meanwhile, fill another saucepan with water, bring it to the boil, reduce the heat to a simmer and cook the sausage for 1 hour.

While the meat is cooking, prepare the sauce. Put the cranberries into a saucepan with the sugar and cook them, covered, for about 10 minutes over a low heat until the juice is syrupy, when a drop poured on to a plate will stay perfectly round – the liquid should have evaporated almost completely. Leave it to cool, then pour it into a bowl. When beef, chicken and veal are ready, drain the pan, reserving the juices, and discard the vegetables and herbs. Drain the sausage. Arrange the meat on a serving platter with a little of the meat juice. Pass round the sauce separately.

GOOSEBERRIES

(RIBES GROSSULARIA)

For those who have never seen a gooseberry, the Italian name is more helpful than the English. *Uva spina* means 'thorn-grape' and tells you that most gooseberries look like grapes that grow on thorny or spiny bushes. They come in a wide range of grape colours, white, yellow, green, red and purple. Most varieties are grape-sized but some are as big as small plums while some have hairy skin.

Why the English, who enjoy them most, call them gooseberries is disputed. My Oxford dictionary admits that it might be because traditionally they were cooked with goose. The seventeenth-century writer Giacomo Castelvetro remarked that 'in recent years' the English nobility had begun to put gooseberries in the sauce they served with goose. He went on to say that Italians liked to revive their jaded palates with sharp tastes and so put sour gooseberries in sauces for chicken, squab and veal. And when gooseberries were not in season they substituted verjuice, the juice of unripe grapes. The French, on the other hand, called gooseberries *groseille à maquereau*, the 'berry for mackerel', as they used them in a sauce for this fish, as oily in its way as goose.

At any rate, botanically the gooseberry is a species of the genus *ribes* or currant. Early-season gooseberries are too sour and hard to eat raw but are good for cooking. Some varieties of midsummer gooseberries can be eaten as a dessert fruit. As a young woman after the Second World War, I visited England and tasted my first gooseberries in gooseberry fool, a delicious dessert which consists of mashed gooseberries, sweetened with lots of sugar and topped with heaps of cream.

GOOSEBERRIES STEWED WITH CARROTS

600G/1¼LB CARROTS, TRIMMED,
PEELED AND DICED
600G/1¼LB GOOSEBERRIES, TOPPED
AND TAILED
2 TBSP EXTRA-VIRGIN OLIVE OIL
60G/2OZ/4 TBSP SUGAR
2 TBSP BALSAMIC VINEGAR
SALT

Bring a large saucepan of water to the boil, immerse the carrots in it for 1 minute, then drain them. Return them to the pan with the gooseberries and the oil, and cook, covered, over a low heat for about 10 minutes or until tender. Stir in the sugar and the balsamic vinegar, season with salt, and cook for a further 5 minutes. This is delicious served with roasted fowl or braised meats.

GOOSEBERRY CREAM

1KG/2LB GOOSEBERRIES, TOPPED AND
TAILED
4 EGG YOLKS AND 2 EGG WHITES
120G/4OZ/½ CUP SUGAR
240ML/8FL OZ/1 CUP MILK

Reserve a few of the gooseberries for decoration, purée the rest in a blender, then push them through a sieve. Discard the seeds. Beat the egg yolks with the sugar, then stir in the milk and the gooseberry purée. Pour the mixture into the top half of a double-boiler, or set the mixing bowl over a pan of simmering water, then cook over a medium heat, stirring continuously, until the custard coats the back of a spoon. Do not let it boil. Let it cool completely, stirring from time to time to prevent a skin forming. Beat the egg whites stiffly and fold them into the custard. Pour the gooseberry cream into a serving bowl, decorate with the reserved gooseberries and chill until you are ready to serve.

GOOSEBERRIES IN CHAMPAGNE

600G/1¼LB GOOSEBERRIES, TOPPED
AND TAILED
1 HALF-BOTTLE CHAMPAGNE OR
SPARKLING WINE
90G/3OZ/6 TBSP SUGAR
240ML/8FL OZ/1 CUP DOUBLE
(HEAVY) CREAM

Put the gooseberries in a bowl, cover
them with the champagne and let them
stand for 2 hours at room temperature.
Drain, then add the sugar to the gooseberries. Whip the cream to soft peaks
and fold in the gooseberries. Chill until
you are ready to serve.

81

BLACKCURRANTS

(RIBES NIGRUM)

I HAVE THE IMPRESSION that currants are to Europe what blueberries are to North America. When we go berry picking, at least in Italy, it is usually currants we are after. They grow wild everywhere and in great profusion. I have read that currants are the second most cultivated soft fruit in the world, after the strawberry.

All currants are of the *ribes* family, including gooseberries. Although currants have been used since medieval times, especially in Scandinavia, they were not widely cultivated in Europe until the seventeenth century. In Italy blackcurrants are also referred to as mountain currants (*ribes di monte*), because they are the dominant species of wild currant. They grow on bramble bushes that flower in spring and produce clusters of berries in the summer. You can catch their aroma from a distance and their flavour is sour and aromatic. They are best eaten cooked and are used in sorbets and fruit puddings.

Blackcurrants were valued in folk medicine, especially as a cure for colds. I remember as a child being given blackcurrant cough medicine. The French make a liqueur from blackcurrants, *cassis*, which has been popularized worldwide in the cocktail known as Kir, named after a Resistance hero from Dijon, Monsieur Kir, which consists of a drop of *cassis* in dry white wine. A Kir Royale is made with champagne.

BLACKCURRANT AND BARLEY SOUP

210G/7OZ BARLEY
600ML/1¼ PT/3 CUPS SKIMMED MILK
120G/4OZ/½ CUP SUGAR
300G/10OZ/1½ CUPS BLACKCURRANTS,
TOPPED AND TAILED
6 SLICES PANETTONE

Put the barley and the milk into a saucepan and bring it to the boil. Turn down the heat and cook for about 1 hour, or until the barley is tender. Stir in the sugar and the blackcurrants and keep it warm. Toast the panettone slices on both sides until they are just golden. Lay 1 piece in each serving bowl then pour over the soup and serve.

BLACKCURRANT MOUSSE

600G/1¼LB BLACKCURRANTS
120G/4OZ/½ CUP SUGAR
240ML/8OZ/1 CUP DOUBLE
(HEAVY) CREAM

Rinse the blackcurrants in cold water and place in a large pan. Cover and cook on a very low heat for about 5 minutes, or until tender. Add the sugar, mix gently with the softened blackcurrants and allow to cool completely.

Whip the cream until soft peaks form and then fold into the blackcurrant purée. Arrange in a bowl and chill before serving.

BLACKCURRANT SORBET

900G/30OZ/4½ CUPS BLACKCURRANTS
240G/8OZ/1 CUP SUGAR
120ML/4FL OZ/½ CUP WATER
JUICE OF 1 LEMON
1 EGG WHITE, BEATEN UNTIL STIFF

Rinse the blackcurrants and place in a saucepan and cover. Cook on a low heat for a few minutes, or until tender. Pass through a sieve, pressing hard so that all the juice comes through. Set aside. Boil the sugar and water for about 5 minutes or until syrupy (a drop on a flat surface will stay round). Add to the blackcurrant purée with the lemon juice and allow to cool completely. Place in an ice-cream machine and freeze according to instructions. Alternatively place in the freezer for about 4 hours, stirring occasionally to break up the ice crystals. In both cases add the beaten egg white 10 minutes before the final setting of the sorbet.

REDCURRANTS

(RIBES RUBRUM)

ALTHOUGH REDCURRANTS have been used in cooking since medieval times, especially in Scandinavia, they were not widely cultivated in Europe until the seventeenth century. They grow on deciduous bushes that are trained into hedges five to six feet tall. Their lovely scarlet berries became a favourite subject for northern European still life painters. Today their decorative value is appreciated by restaurant cooks who often use the bright jewel-like berries to garnish both sweet and savoury dishes. Translucent 'white' currants are a colourless offshoot of the redcurrants. Sometimes, you see an in-between berry that is a pretty pink.

These currants, especially the white, are less tart than the blackcurrant and can be eaten on their own – with a generous sprinkling of sugar. They can also be used to give a pleasingly tart flavour and beautiful colour to sauces for meat dishes and desserts. Redcurrant jelly is a classic example. Redcurrants are often used with other, sweeter berries such as raspberries and strawberries in summer fruit puddings. In markets you often see little boxes with all three colours mixed. They can be cooked together. In England, they are the main ingredient in a classic dessert aptly named summer pudding.

REDCURRANT OMELETTE

6 LARGE EGGS
180G/6OZ/⅔ CUP SUGAR
180ML/6FL OZ/⅔ CUP DOUBLE
(HEAVY) CREAM
30G/1OZ/2 TBSP UNSALTED BUTTER
180ML/6FL OZ/⅔ CUP YOGURT
600G/20OZ/3 CUPS REDCURRANTS,
TOPPED, TAILED, STALKS REMOVED

Preheat the oven to 200°C/400°F/gas mark 6.

Beat the eggs separately in 6 small bowls (or prepare 2 or 3 at a time) with ½ tablespoon each of the sugar and 1 tablespoon each of cream. Divide the butter into 6. Take 1 piece, put it into a small, non-stick frying-pan and let it melt over a medium heat. Pour in a portion of the egg mixture and cook until it is almost set, shaking the pan frequently. Turn the omelette and cook for just 1 minute on the other side. Repeat until you have 6 omelettes. Stir together the rest of the sugar, the yogurt and the redcurrants, then use this to fill the omelettes. Roll them up and lay them in an ovenproof dish. Heat them through in the oven for 5 minutes, then serve immediately.

REDCURRANT CHAMPAGNE CUP

300G/10OZ/1½ CUPS REDCURRANTS,
TOPPED, TAILED, STALKS REMOVED
90G/3OZ/6 TBSP SUGAR
1 BOTTLE DRY CHAMPAGNE

Rinse the redcurrants and place in a large punch bowl. Sprinkle with the sugar and pour over the champagne. Chill in the refrigerator so that the flavours become mingled. Do not chill for more than 2 hours or the champagne will go flat. This champagne cup is a perfect aperitif for a summer celebration party.

WHITECURRANT RICE MOULD

210G/7OZ/1 CUP ARBORIO RICE
480ML/16FL OZ/2 CUPS MILK
4 LARGE EGG YOLKS
240G/8OZ/1 CUP SUGAR
300G/10OZ/1¼ CUPS WHITECURRANTS,
TOPPED, TAILED AND STALKS
REMOVED
90G/3OZ/6 TBSP BUTTER, MELTED,
EXTRA BUTTER, FOR GREASING
120ML/4FL OZ/½ CUP DOUBLE
(HEAVY) CREAM

Preheat the oven to 175°C/350°F gas mark 4.

Bring a saucepan of water to the boil, put in the rice and cook over a medium heat for about 5 minutes, then drain. Pour the milk into the saucepan, add the rice and cook over a low heat, stirring frequently, until the milk has been absorbed, about 20 minutes. Leave it to cool. Stir in the egg yolks, the sugar, the whitecurrants, melted butter and cream. Butter a 1.5-litre (3-pt) baking-dish, pour in the rice mixture and cover it with foil. Set it in a bain-marie, containing around 2.5cm (1in) water, and bake for about 1 hour or until firm. Leave it to cool a little. To turn out, slide the point of a knife around the edge of the pudding to loosen it, then invert the dish over a serving platter. Serve either warm or at room temperature with a little raspberry sauce *(see page 60)*.

CURRANT COMPOTE

900G/30OZ/4½ CUPS CURRANTS,
TOPPED, TAILED, STALKS REMOVED
90G/3OZ/6 TBSP SUGAR
JUICE OF 1 LEMON

Rinse the currants and arrange them in a bowl. Sprinkle with the sugar and add the lemon juice. Chill in the refrigerator until ready to serve. Mix gently and serve with yogurt, ice-cream or simply mixed cream.

MEDITERRANEAN
FRUIT

FIGS

(FICUS CARICA)

> '*Full on its crown, a fig's green branches rise
> And shoot a leafy forest to the skies.*'
> (HOMER, ODYSSEY, BK XIII)

FIGS, OLIVES AND GRAPES are the three elemental fruits of the Mediterranean. As if to prove just how fundamental they are to this area, fig seeds take root everywhere and anywhere, in the tiniest cracks in old stone walls and pavements. You must uproot them quickly or they would soon uproot you. They were here first.

The fig tree probably originated in Asia Minor. It is mentioned in the Book of Genesis and is said to have grown in the Garden of Eden. Its large leaves came in handy when Adam and Eve got into trouble and puritanical popes used them to cover human nakedness on many Roman statues. Some of the world's most delicious figs still come from the Middle East, in particular Smyrna figs from Izmir in Turkey. Today this once exotic fruit is produced as far from its native land as California and Brazil.

The pear-shaped or oval fig is a pulpy receptacle containing many minute flowers and undeveloped fruits, which account for that characteristic crunch when you bite into it. Centuries of propagation have produced hundreds of varieties – botanists count more than 700 in Italy alone – with varying characteristics. It is easiest to classify them according to two basic colours: white, with hues ranging from pale green to dark gold, and red, which varies from burnished brown to a deep purple that can appear almost black. Some of the most popular figs you are likely to see in Italian markets are the Dottato (sometimes called Ottato), the Gentile Bianco (a white fig), the Genovese, the Verdello and the Brogiollo Nero and Bianco.

In Italy figs bear two crops of fruit each year. The first is produced from June to July from the previous season's buds and are called fiorone. These figs are large and juicy, especially when it has been a rainy spring, but almost tasteless. The second crop is the true fig, produced from this season's growth and ripening from late August to October. These figs are small and delicate in flavour. The taste of some varieties remind me of honey and others of berry jam.

Absolutely and unquestionably the best way to eat a fig is ripe off the tree, ideally still warm from the sun. Since the ripe fruit is delicate and does not travel well, it is difficult but not impossible, especially if you are shopping in a fig-growing area, to find a perfectly mature fig. You should look for fruit with thin, unblemished skin. Sun-ripened figs will often have little beads of moisture coming from the top. If you are buying figs in their country of origin and plan on eating them immediately, don't worry about split skins. One of Italy's classical seasonal sweet and savoury dishes is sun-ripened spring figs with prosciutto. Dried figs are produced from the autumn crop and are traditionally served during the Christmas holidays.

FIG AND TUNA SKEWERS

6 TUNA STEAKS, ABOUT 240G/8OZ
EACH
4 TBSP EXTRA-VIRGIN OLIVE OIL
SALT AND PEPPER
12 FIGS
24 BAY LEAVES

Preheat the oven to 200°C/400°F/gas mark 6.

Divide the tuna steaks into 4 pieces each and trim them neatly. Heat 3 tablespoons of the oil in a frying-pan, then put in the tuna and sauté over a high heat for 2 minutes. Season to taste with salt and pepper, drain and reserve. Cut the figs in half vertically, keeping the skin on. Take 6 skewers and alternate 4 pieces of tuna with 4 fig halves and 4 bay leaves. Brush a baking-dish with the rest of the oil, arrange the skewers in it and bake for 10 minutes, turning the skewers once. Serve immediately, very hot.

FUSILLI WITH BACON AND FIGS

600G/1¼LB FUSILLI, OR
PENNE OR RIGATONI
SALT
120G/4OZ SMOKED BACON, DICED
1 SMALL ONION, PEELED AND CHOPPED
9 FIGS, QUARTERED
2 TBSP EXTRA-VIRGIN OLIVE OIL
6 SLICES PARMA HAM, SLICED PAPER-
THIN, THEN ROUGHLY CHOPPED

Bring a saucepan of salted water to the boil, then put in the pasta. Meanwhile fry the bacon in little oil in a heavy frying-pan with the onion until the onion is translucent and the bacon crisp – about 5 minutes. Add the figs and sauté for a couple of minutes. When the fusilli is cooked al dente, drain it and put it in a bowl with the rest of the oil, stir, then add the bacon, onion and fig mixture. Scatter over the Parma ham and serve immediately.

Make sure that your pasta is cooked just al dente by boiling it for a couple of minutes less than the time given on the packet then testing it. Pasta is more digestible when slightly undercooked.

FIG TART

240G/8OZ READY-MADE PUFF PASTRY
480G/1LB FRESH RIPE FIGS
2-3 TBSP CLEAR HONEY
YOGURT, CREAM OR CREME FRAICHE

FOR THE FRANGIPANE
60G/2OZ/4 TBSP BUTTER
60G/2OZ/4 TBSP SUGAR
60G/2OZ/4 TBSP GROUND ALMONDS
1 EGG
3 DROPS OF ALMOND ESSENCE

Preheat the oven to 175°C/350°F/gas mark 4.

Roll out the pastry and use to line a 20 x 30-cm (8 x 12-in) oblong tart tin. Bake blind until just golden. Wash the figs, pat dry and slice in half. Meanwhile make the frangipane by placing the butter, sugar and ground almonds in a food processor and process until the ingredients are combined. Add the egg and almond essence and work until the mixture becomes a smooth paste. Spread the frangipane inside the cooked pastry shell, making sure it is level and smooth. Arrange the figs in rows on top of the frangipane.

Bake in the oven for 45-60 minutes. Melt the honey gently in a pan and brush the top of the figs to glaze. Return to the oven for a further five minutes. Serve warm with yogurt, cream or crème fraîche.

GRAPES

(VITIS VINIFERA)

'On foreign mountains may the sun refine
The grape's soft juice, and mellow it to wine.'
(ADDISON, A LETTER FROM ITALY, 1704)

HUMANKIND HAS HAD a longer gastronomic relationship with grapes than with any other fruit. Archaeologists have discovered that long before Noah planted his vineyard on the slopes of Mount Ararat, wild grapes were flourishing in the Caucasus, which would seem to be their land of origin. Tomb paintings in Luxor's Valley of the Kings show Egyptians at work cultivating vines and making wine, and ancient Greek and Roman history is replete with accounts of wine-making and wine-drinking. Today Italy is third among countries with areas planted in vineyards, after Spain and the former Soviet Union, but it is ranked first for grape varieties and volume of wine produced. My family are wine-producers so my relationship with the grape has always been close.

Grape varieties must number over a hundred. Some are cultivated exclusively for wine, some for eating at the table, while others are grown for drying into raisins, sultanas and currants. For practical purposes they all fall into the general division according to skin colour of white or red. Some white grapes are more truly yellow and green, while reds are often so deep a purple they are called black. Their colour, of course, is only skin deep: the flesh of all grapes is translucent. Some skins have a naturally shiny, almost waxy surface, while others show a delicate powdery deposit called bloom.

In years past I could find a wide variety of table grapes in the local market from July to December. Unfortunately a number of our native varieties, such as the flavourful Cardinal and the sweet Regina, are in danger of becoming extinct due to the appeal of seedless exports to undiscerning palates. Seedless grapes contain less tannin and therefore have less flavour than seeded fruit. I think the most delicious still thriving Italian table grape is the Italia, a white grape with large seeds and a pleasing crunch to the skin that releases a sweet juice. It is popular on the Christmas table, although expensive in late December, as in cold weather the vines have to be covered.

Both for eating fresh and for incorporating into other dishes, some of the most delicious grapes are those classified as dessert varieties. Italy is the world's largest producer of dessert grapes. King of this category is the marvellously fragrant and honey-flavoured Moscato. Apart from wine, Italian gastronomy has created another nectar using grape juice, the ineffable *balsamico*, made from unfermented grape must and aged for generations in small casks of various woods. Often wine vinegar is added to *balsamico* to make *aceto balsamico*. Until, however, you have tasted the real condiment (sometimes labelled as *aceto balsamico tradizionale*) you have not yet had a taste of paradise.

GRAPES AND ONIONS IN SWEET AND SOUR SAUCE

2 TBSP EXTRA-VIRGIN OLIVE OIL

30G/1OZ/2 TBSP UNSALTED BUTTER

300G/1OOZ PEARL ONIONS, PEELED
AND TRIMMED

SALT AND PEPPER

90G/3OZ/6 TBSP BROWN SUGAR

60ML/2FL OZ/¼ CUP RED WINE VINEGAR

210G/7OZ WHITE GRAPES

210G/7OZ RED GRAPES

Heat the oil and the butter in a frying-pan, add the onions and sauté over a low heat for about 10 minutes, covered. Season with salt and pepper, then add the sugar and the vinegar. Cook, uncovered, for 10 more minutes, or until the vinegar has evaporated, then add the grapes and continue to cook for 5 more minutes. Serve warm. You can peel, halve and seed the grapes if you like, but I think that if you do the finished dish will be less tasty and colourful.

GRAPE AND CHEESE SALAD

300G/1OOZ GRAPES

210G/7OZ GOAT'S CHEESE

150G/5OZ ROCKET

SALT AND PEPPER

4 TBSP EXTRA-VIRGIN OLIVE OIL

Arrange the grapes on a platter. Dice the cheese and scatter it over and around the grapes, then distribute the rocket over the top and around the edges. Sprinkle with salt and pepper, drizzle over the olive oil and serve at room temperature – refrigeration takes away the aroma.

SMOKED TROUT FILLETS WITH GRAPES

6 SMOKED TROUT FILLETS, ABOUT
210G/7OZ EACH

90G/3OZ/6 TBSP PLAIN (ALL-PURPOSE)
FLOUR

480G/16OZ GRAPES

60G/2OZ/4 TBSP UNSALTED BUTTER

2 TBSP EXTRA-VIRGIN OLIVE OIL

SALT

Trim the trout fillets, coat them with flour and shake off the excess. Squeeze a quarter of the grapes, reserving the juice. Heat the butter and the oil in a frying-pan, add the trout fillets and sauté over a medium heat for 3 minutes on each side. Add the grape juice and the remaining grapes, then cook for 5 more minutes, or until the juice has almost evaporated. Check the seasoning and adjust if necessary, then serve immediately.

ORANGES

(CITRUS SINENSIS)

'Yes, sing the song of the orange-tree
With its leaves of velvet green,
With its luscious fruit of sunset hue,
The fairest that ever were seen.'

(J K HOYT, THE ORANGE TREE)

IN LATE MEDIEVAL and early Renaissance times oranges were a symbol of wealth and power. To get that point across, my Florentine ancestors, who were big-time bankers, put five on their coat-of-arms. In those days the orange was an exotic rarity. Originally it came from China, but the Arabs brought it to southern Europe at the beginning of the eleventh century. In her *Fruit Book*, Jane Grigson notes that it came to us via the Persians from an Indian word meaning 'perfume within'.

All those ancient oranges would have been too bitter to eat. They were what is known today as the Seville orange, *citrus aurantium*. They were valued for the decorative effect of their trees, laden with aromatic blossoms and brightly coloured fragrant fruit. A lovely distillation was made from the blossom and used as a scent to perfume bath and body. The fruit was put into preserves, candied, and the juice used as a flavouring. The sweet orange was not introduced to Europe until the seventeenth century, brought from India by Portuguese explorers. Cultivation on a large scale began almost a century later.

In Italy you will find two principal types of oranges in the market, the blond and the blood. The blond, with pale to deep yellow flesh, includes common varieties such as the navel and the Valencia, and an Italian type called Calabrese. I think blood oranges are by far the most interesting. The first variety to arrive in November from the south of Italy, Calabria, Puglia and Sicily, is the Moro, a large fruit with deep red flesh and a slight red blush on the rind. These are followed in December by the Tarocco, with a lighter interior and exterior red colour. The most beautiful variety, the Sanguinello, arrives last. Its name means 'lovely little blood-coloured' orange. It has red flesh and red-flushed skin. When squeezed it yields a splendid ruby red juice. Some years ago, when blood oranges were not well known outside the southern Mediterranean, it was not unusual to hear visitors from abroad say to their waiter at breakfast, 'Please take this tomato juice back. We ordered orange.'

Like lemons, oranges are a versatile fruit in the kitchen. Each component, skin oil, rind, zest, juice and flesh, adds colour, aroma and flavour to innumerable dishes.

ORANGE, FENNEL AND ONION SALAD

3 ORANGES, PEELED, PITH REMOVED
2 FENNEL BULBS, TRIMMED
1 RED ONION, PEELED
12 BLACK OLIVES, GAETA OR GREEK,
PITTED
SALT AND PEPPER
4 TBSP EXTRA-VIRGIN OLIVE OIL

Slice the oranges. Then slice the fennel bulbs lengthwise and the onion paper-thin. Arrange the orange slices on a platter, alternating them with the fennel. Scatter over the onion, decorate with the olives and season with salt and pepper. Pour over the olive oil and serve at room temperature – do not keep this salad in the refrigerator as the oranges will release too much juice.

ORANGE AND ONION RICE

2 LARGE WHITE ONIONS, PEELED AND
FINELY CHOPPED
90G/3OZ/6 TBSP UNSALTED BUTTER
1½ LITRES/3PT/6 CUPS CHICKEN STOCK
720G/24OZ/3 CUPS LONG-GRAIN RICE
ZEST OF 2 ORANGES
SALT AND PEPPER

Sauté the onions in half of the butter over a low heat until they are translucent, about 3 minutes. Bring the stock to the boil. Add the rice and the onion, stir well and when it is hot, after about 3 minutes, pour in the stock, add the orange zest, then cover and cook for about 15 minutes, or until the rice is al dente. Add the rest of the butter, season with salt and pepper, stir well, take the pan off the heat and let it rest for a minute before serving This is a delicious accompaniment to stewed lamb or chicken.

ORANGE SABAYON

6 LARGE EGG YOLKS
180G/6OZ/⅞ CUP SUGAR
300ML/10FL OZ/1¼ CUPS ORANGE
JUICE
240ML/8FL OZ/1 CUP DOUBLE
(HEAVY) CREAM
WILD STRAWBERRIES TO
SERVE (OPTIONAL)

Whisk the egg yolks with the sugar, then stir in the orange juice. Pour the mixture into the top half of a double-boiler, or set the mixing bowl over a pan of simmering water, then cook, whisking continuously, until the custard thickens and coats the whisk. Don't let it boil. Then whisk it over iced water until it is cold. Whip the cream stiffly, then fold it into the orange mixture. (This also makes a delicious ice-cream: see page 120 for instructions on how to freeze it.) Pour the sabayon into 6 champagne flutes and serve chilled, accompanied by wild strawberries, when available.

LEMONS

(CITRUS LIMONUM)

'*Know you the land where the lemon-trees bloom?*'

(Goethe, Wilhelm Meisters Lehrjahre, III, I, 1795-6)

For northern europeans the country of the lemon tree is Italy. For Italians it is more particularly the Amalfi coast and the island of Sicily. For everyone, perhaps, no fruit evokes the Mediterranean as vividly as the lemon – lemon orchards planted on cliffs overhanging the sea, blossoming lemon trees and bright yellow fruit hanging heavy on the branch. Someone, I can't remember who, wrote that she would not want to live more than a few minutes' walk from the nearest lemon tree. I feel myself a kindred spirit. Even in northern, inland Tuscany, where I live, we have potted lemon trees in the garden – about eight, precious family heirlooms. We have to be careful to get them inside before the first autumn frost and to resist the temptation to take them out too quickly after the first (deceitful) sunny days of spring. Then there is the lemon's association with the food and drink of the Mediterranean, the fruit of the land lending flavour and zest to the fruits of the sea, providing refreshing drinks and sorbets taken in the heat of the afternoon and finally a glass of chilled limoncello on a balmy summer evening.

The lemon tree originally came from India. The ancient Egyptians cultivated it and it is thought that Alexander the Great brought it from Persia to Greece. The lemon probably came to Italy and the rest of southern Europe with the Arab invasions in the ninth century. Today 90 per cent of all Italy's production comes from Sicily, which was under Arab rule for almost three centuries. The island's climate encourages trees to yield up to three crops a year, in early spring, summer and autumn.

I can think of no more useful fruit than the lemon. Its skin contains aromatic essential oils so has innumerable culinary uses, either finely grated as zest or cut into strips. The juice makes a refreshing drink or enhances the flavour of other foods. Slices and wedges of the fruit are indispensable to fish dishes and with fried foods to cut the oily taste. The whole fruit can be used in dozens of sweet or savoury dishes, from pasta to pastry.

Buy fresh, organic lemons. If you are only familiar with the waxed ones, the fragrance of a real lemon will come as a revelation and its flavour will thrill your tastebuds.

LEMON SOUP

3 LARGE EGGS
ZEST AND JUICE OF 3 LEMONS
1.5 L/2½PT/6 CUPS CHICKEN STOCK
180G/6OZ/6 TBSP COARSE SEMOLINA
SALT AND PEPPER
1 TBSP FINELY CHOPPED FLAT-LEAF
PARSLEY

Break the eggs into a bowl, add the lemon juice, stir well and set aside. Add the lemon zest to the chicken stock, bring it to the boil, then turn down the heat and simmer for a few minutes. Stir the semolina into the egg mixture, then whisk in the stock. Pour the soup back into the saucepan, season with salt and pepper, then cook for a couple of minutes over a medium heat. Turn off the heat, sprinkle the parsley over and serve immediately.

LEMON RICOTTA TART

FOR THE PASTRY
180G/6OZ/1¼ CUPS PLAIN (ALL-
PURPOSE) FLOUR
120G/4OZ/½ CUP COARSE SEMOLINA
120G/4OZ/8 TBSP UNSALTED BUTTER,
DICED, PLUS EXTRA FOR GREASING
120G/4OZ/½ CUP SUGAR
1 LARGE EGG YOLK
2 TBSP MILK

FOR THE FILLING
1 WHOLE EGG PLUS 1 YOLK
240G/8OZ/1 CUP RICOTTA
60G/2OZ/4 TBSP ICING-SUGAR
GRATED ZEST OF 1 LEMON
10 DROPS LEMON ESSENCE
120ML/4OZ/½ CUP DOUBLE CREAM

Preheat the oven to 175°C/350°F/gas mark 4.

Put the flour, semolina, butter, sugar, egg yolk and milk into a food processor and process until a dough forms. Wrap it in clingfilm and put it into the refrigerator for about 1 hour. Butter a 25-cm (10-in) diameter tart tin. Roll out the dough and use it to line the tin. Bake it until it is golden, about 20 minutes. There is no need to use baking beans – if the pastry bubbles up during cooking, remove from the oven, flatten it again with the palm of your hand and return to the oven to finish cooking.

Meanwhile, make the filling. Mix the egg and egg yolk with the ricotta, then add the icing-sugar, the lemon zest and essence. Whisk the cream to soft peaks, then fold it into the ricotta mixture. Pour the filling into the cooked pastry case and bake for about 20 minutes or until it is golden. Decorate with caramelized lemon peel, if desired.

LEMON CURD

MAKES APPROXIMATELY 600G/1¼LB
10 LEMONS
10 LARGE EGG YOLKS
980G/2LB/4 CUPS SUGAR
300G/10OZ/1¼ CUPS UNSALTED
BUTTER

Squeeze the lemons, then strain and reserve the juice. Beat the egg yolks with the sugar until creamy, then add the butter and the lemon juice and continue to beat until fluffy. Pour the mixture into the top half of a double-boiler, or set the mixing bowl over a pan of simmering water and whisk continuously – do not let it boil – until it coats the back of a spoon. Pour it into warmed, sterilized glass jars and seal. The lemon curd will keep in the refrigerator for up to 3 months.

GRAPEFRUIT

(CITRUS PARADISI)

GRAPEFRUIT WERE NOT KNOWN IN ITALY until the nineteenth century when they arrived from Florida. Their native land is Malaysia.

I ate my first grapefruit in England, when I visited London shortly after the Second World War. I remember there was a special silver spoon with a sharp tip and serrated edge to cut out the wedges of flesh. I didn't see a grapefruit tree until many years later when I was in Southern California. Only relatively recently has the grapefruit taken root in Italy and now it is cultivated in Sicily and Calabria.

Grapefruit tends to grow in grape-like clusters on the branches of its large tree, thus its English name. The French *pamplemousse* literally means 'a pumpkin-sized citron' and in Italy grapefruit is called *pompelmo*, from *pomelo*, another citrus fruit to which it is related. Several varieties of grapefruit are available. Most have yellow skins and their flesh ranges from pale yellow through deepening shades of pink. Usually the pinker ones are the less tart in taste. There is a green-skinned variety called Sweetie, which, as it name implies, is sweet.

Italian recipe books from the fifties explained that 'In Northern Europe the grapefruit is usually eaten at breakfast, sprinkled with sugar.' A friend of mine from California told me that his mother, as a Sunday breakfast treat, would sprinkle a grapefruit half with brown sugar and put it under the grill for a few minutes until it caramelized. I quite like its natural sweet-sour taste and don't find it needs to be sweetened artificially. In the kitchen I sometimes use grapefruit as a refreshingly pleasant change in recipes that would normally call for other citrus fruits. It is also one of the richest sources of vitamins among citrus fruit, with A and B, as well as C.

GRAPEFRUIT MERINGUE

3 PINK GRAPEFRUIT, PEELED, PITH
REMOVED
4 LARGE EGGS, SEPARATED
120G/4OZ/½ CUP SUGAR
30G/1OZ/2 TBSP PLAIN (ALL-PURPOSE)
FLOUR
480ML/16FL OZ/2 CUPS MILK
60G/2OZ SLICED ALMONDS

With a sharp knife, cut the grapefruit into segments, discarding the membrane. Beat the egg yolks with the sugar and the flour until smooth, stir in the milk and pour the mixture into the top half of a double-boiler, or set the mixing bowl over a pan of simmering water. Cook, stirring all the time with a wooden spoon, until the mixture thickens and starts to bubble. Take it off the heat and leave it to cool, stirring from time to time to prevent a skin forming. Beat the egg whites until they form stiff peaks, then fold them gently into the custard. Heat the grill. Spoon half of the meringue mixture into an ovenproof dish, lay the grapefruit segments over it, then top with the rest of the meringue. Sprinkle over the sliced almonds, then place the dish under the grill for a few minutes until the surface is bubbling and has turned golden brown. Serve immediately.

GRAPEFRUIT COMPOTE

6 GRAPEFRUIT
240G/8OZ/1 CUP SUGAR
480ML/16OZ/2 CUPS RED WINE

Remove the zest from 1 grapefruit and put it into a saucepan with the sugar and the wine. Bring it to the boil and simmer for 20 minutes, or until the liquid is syrupy – a drop on a saucer will remain round and firm. Peel the rest of the grapefruit with a sharp knife, removing all pith, and cut it into segments, discarding the membrane. Arrange the grapefruit in a bowl, cover it with the wine syrup and put it in the refrigerator.

GRAPEFRUIT AND OLIVE SALAD

2 WHITE GRAPEFRUIT, PEELED, PITH
REMOVED
1 RED GRAPEFRUIT, PEELED, PITH
REMOVED
6 GREEN OLIVES
6 TBSP GIN
FRESHLY GROUND BLACK PEPPER

With a sharp knife, cut the grapefruit into segments, discarding the membrane. Place in a bowl with the olives and sprinkle with the gin. Season with pepper and place in the refrigerator until ready to serve. Pink or red grapefruit, with their sweeter flavour and pretty colour, are better suited for this recipe. This is a very pleasant appetizer for warm summer evenings.

PERSIMMONS

(DIOSPYROS KAKI)

'The Persimmon doth hard and bitter stay
Until there come a truly frosty day.'
(AMERICAN PROVERB)

IN THE FIELDS AND VALLEYS of Tuscany in December you will see leafless trees illuminated by reddish-gold bulbs, like so many rustic Christmas trees. These are persimmons, a relatively new addition to the landscape. Originally they came from Japan and it is the Japanese persimmon that is now cultivated in the Mediterranean. It is of the species *Diospyros kaki*, whose name means 'food of the gods', and there is something divine about its glowing golden colour, luscious orange-red flesh, like the robes of a Buddhist monk, and its deliciously sweet, mildly spicy flavour.

However, persimmons are one of those things you either like or you don't. It is not a fruit I long for out of season, like figs, for example, but I do look forward to tasting it again every autumn. In north-central Italy persimmons begin to ripen so late in the year that they have to be picked before they are fully ripe, usually in late autumn, then left to mature off the tree. The perfect fruit has an almost transparent skin and looks as if it is ready to burst, which it often does before you get it home from the market. This is no problem as long as you eat it right away. The flesh is very soft and gelatinous.

A type of persimmon developed in the Sharon Valley of Israel, and called the Sharon fruit, is sweeter than the Oriental persimmon and can be eaten while it is still somewhat underripe. The American persimmon (*Diospyros virginiana*) can also be dried like a fig or apricot. The English word 'persimmon' is derived from the Native American Algonquin word meaning 'dried fruit'.

The easiest and one of the best ways to enjoy a ripe persimmon is simply to cut off the top and scoop out the flesh with a spoon. I find it cries out for a squeeze of lemon or better yet a little lime. A Japanese friend and neighbour in Tuscany remembers from her childhood eating a persimmon off the tree in the dead of winter. Its juicy pulp was frozen solid, like an exotic ice lolly.

PERSIMMON AND PECORINO CHEESE APPETIZER

540G/1LB 2OZ PECORINO, SLICED
INTO 6
2 PERSIMMONS, PEELED
1 HANDFUL FRESH MINT LEAVES

Peel away and discard the pecorino rind, then grill the slices until golden, about 5 minutes on each side. Purée the persimmons in a blender. Arrange the cheese slices, still very warm, on 6 dessert plates, spoon over the persimmon purée, scatter on the mint and serve immediately.

PERSIMMON PARFAIT

4 LARGE EGG YOLKS
90G/3OZ/6 TBSP SUGAR
480ML/16FL OZ/2 CUPS MILK
15G/½OZ GELATINE LEAVES OR
CRYSTALS
240ML/6FL OZ/¾ CUP DOUBLE
(HEAVY) CREAM
4 PERSIMMONS, PEELED

Whisk together the egg yolks and the sugar, then stir in the milk and transfer the mixture to the top half of a double-boiler, or set the mixing bowl over a saucepan of simmering water, and cook, whisking continuously, until the custard coats the back of the spoon. Meanwhile, put the gelatine leaves into a bowl, cover them with water and leave them to soften for 10 minutes, or melt the crystals following the instructions on the packet. Squeeze out the excess liquid, then add the gelatine to the custard and stir, off the heat, until it has dissolved. Allow the mixture to cool. Beat the cream until stiff, then fold into the custard. Purée the persimmons in a blender, then fold the pulp carefully into the custard until it is well blended. Wet a 1.2-litre (2-pt) bowl and pour in the persimmon parfait. Leave it in the refrigerator for at least 4 hours. To serve, loosen the parfait around the edge with a knife, then invert the bowl and turn it out on to a serving dish.

PERSIMMON AND MASCARPONE PUDDINGS

600G/1¼LB MASCARPONE
90G/3OZ/6 TBSP SUGAR
1 TSP POWDERED CINNAMON
1 TBSP ALMOND OIL
4 PERSIMMONS, PEELED

Cream the mascarpone with a wooden spoon until it is smooth, then stir in the sugar and the cinnamon. Brush 6 individual moulds or ramekins with the oil, then fill them with the mascarpone mixture. Level the surface and chill. Purée the persimmons in a blender. To serve, turn out the moulds into 6 dessert dishes and pour the persimmon purée around the mascarpone puddings.

MELONS

(CUCUMIS MELO)

SWEET MELONS WERE FIRST cultivated on a large scale in the sixteenth century on the estate of the Pope at Cantalupo outside of Rome. These cantaloupes, with their characteristic craggy pale yellowish-green rind sectioned into wedges, were the melons most often depicted by seventeenth-century still-life painters. Today they have become the most popular melon in Europe and America. Long before the papal gardeners began to grow cantaloupes, Italians were eating other sweet melons, which botanists say originally came from China. So fond was Tiberius Caesar of melons that he had special greenhouses built so he could enjoy them all year around.

Over the centuries hundreds of varieties of melon of all shapes and sizes have been developed. They all belong to the botanical family of gourds, producing trailing vines, called Cucurbitaceae, which includes vegetables such as cucumbers and squashes as well as fruit. What they have in common is a hard, attractively patterned rind to protect their soft, juicy flesh.

In the market you find melons both in winter and summer. Winter melons usually have smooth skin and pale flesh with little flavour. Of these, the honeydew is the most common. Summer melons are aromatic with sweet, juicy flesh. Besides the cantaloupe the other most popular Italian melon is the *retato*, or 'netted' melon, so-called because of the net pattern on the rind. It is related to the Galia and Ogen melons and has golden skin and fragrant greenish-yellow flesh. The Tuscan word for melon is popone, which I like, because the sound fits the fruit.

Choosing the perfectly ripe melon is something of an art. Giacomo Castelvetro, the seventeenth-century writer on Italian fruits and vegetables, mentions that in his day the gentlemen of Modena preferred to select melons for themselves and would leave them at the shop for the servant to collect and carry home. My greengrocer, who does not like customers to handle his produce, takes one in each hand to judge their weight. The heavier one should be the best. It is a reliable sign of maturity to find the stalk end soft to the touch. If it smells fragrant that usually settles the question for me. A bit of local folk wisdom: the 'male ' of the species, recognizable by a little black dot at the end opposite the stalk, is considered the superior fruit.

Melons go well with various sweet and savoury ingredients. One of those perfect culinary pairings is prosciutto and melon. These two ingredients can also be incorporated into a delicious and refreshing summer pasta dish, served at room temperature, and flavoured with sprigs of mint.

WATERMELONS

(CITRULLUS VULGARIS)

*'S*tumbling *on melons, as I pass,*
Ensnared with flowers, I fall on grass.'
(ANDREW MARVELL, THE GARDEN, 1681)

SYNONYMOUS WITH SUMMER in Italy are the piles of watermelons stacked in pyramids on roadside stands. In the evenings, at the height of the watermelon season in mid-August, families walk or drive to the nearest and socialize with their neighbours while they eat huge slices. As its English name implies, there is so much liquid in the watermelon that eating it is almost like drinking a sweet juice.

We now know that watermelons originally came from Africa, probably the Nile Valley, although for centuries European botanists presumed they were first grown in southern Italy. North African Arabs probably brought the seeds with them to Sicily and the south. The seventeenth-century writer on Italian fruit Giacomo Castelvetro mentions several types of watermelon, including varieties with yellow and white pulp.

In today's markets you will find the standard varieties of red-fleshed watermelon. The three most common are the Charleston Grey, large, oval-shaped with light green dappled skin; the Crimson Sweet, large and round with pale and dark green stripes; and the Sugar Baby, smaller and rounder with very dark green skin and especially intense red, sweet flesh.

A cup of rosy watermelon sorbet is an especially refreshing way to finish a summer luncheon.

MELON WITH MINT

3 MELONS (CANTALOUPE OR
HONEYDEW), ABOUT 480G/16OZ EACH
240ML/8FL OZ/1 CUP WATER
120G/4OZ/½ CUP SUGAR
1 HANDFUL MINT LEAVES
120ML/4FL OZ/½ CUP DOUBLE CREAM

Halve the melons and discard the seeds. Cut out the flesh and dice it. Refill the melon shells with the diced flesh. Bring the water to the boil with the sugar and the mint leaves, then allow it to reduce until it is syrupy when a drop poured on to a plate will stay perfectly round. Discard the mint and allow the syrup to cool. Pour it evenly between the melon cups. Beat the cream stiffly, then spoon it over the melons and leave them to chill.

MELON AND HONEY ICE-CREAM

MAKES APPROX. 1.2 LITRES/2PINTS
4 LARGE EGG YOLKS
120G/4OZ/½ CUP SUGAR
480ML/16FL OZ/2 CUPS MILK
120ML/4FL OZ/½ CUP DOUBLE
(HEAVY) CREAM
1.2KG/2½LB MELON, EITHER GALIA,
CANTALOUPE OR HONEYDEW, HALVED
AND SEEDED
3 TBSP HONEY

Beat together the egg yolks and the sugar until creamy, then stir in the milk a little at a time. Pour the mixture into the top half of a double-boiler, or set the mixing bowl over a pan of simmering water, and cook, stirring all the time with a wooden spoon, until it thickens and is hot but not boiling. Leave it to go cold. Beat the cream stiffly, then fold it into the custard.

Scoop out the melon flesh and pass it through a food mill or sieve. Stir in the honey. Combine the melon mixture thoroughly with the custard, then pour it into an ice-cream machine and follow the manufacturer's instructions. If you do not have a machine, pour the ice-cream mixture into a suitable container and put it into the freezer for at least 4 hours. After the first 30 minutes, take it out and whisk it to break up the ice crystals. Repeat twice more, at half-hourly intervals, then leave the ice-cream until it is firm. This is delicious served with a little nectarine champagne *(see page 30)* or blueberry grappa *(see page 72)* poured over.

MELON WITH THREE CHEESES

3 MELONS (GALIA, CANTALOUPE OR
HONEYDEW), ABOUT 480G/16OZ EACH,
HALVED, SEEDED AND DICED
120ML/4FL OZ/½ CUP VIN SANTO OR
SAUTERNE
60G/2OZ EMMENTAL, DICED
60G/2OZ STILTON, CRUMBLED
60G/2OZ FONTINA, DICED

Divide the melon dice between the melon shells, pour over the wine, then divide the cheese between them. Serve at room temperature.

WATERMELON SORBET

1 WATERMELON, ABOUT 1.2KG/2½LB
JUICE OF 1 LEMON
180G/6OZ/⅔ CUP SUGAR
240ML/8FL OZ/1 CUP WATER
120G/4OZ CHOCOLATE-COVERED
COFFEE BEANS
1 EGG WHITE

Halve the watermelon and scoop out the flesh. Keep one half of the shell. Remove and discard the seeds then purée the flesh with the lemon juice in a blender. Put the sugar and water into a saucepan and cook over a low heat until it is syrupy, when a drop poured on to a plate remains perfectly round. Allow the syrup to cool, then stir it into the watermelon purée. Add the coffee beans. Pour the mixture into an ice-cream machine and follow the manufacturer's instructions. A few minutes before the sorbet is completely set, whisk the egg white stiffly, then add it to the sorbet mixture. Continue to freeze. When it is ready, pour the sorbet into the reserved half watermelon shell and either serve immediately or store in the freezer until needed. If you do not have an ice-cream machine, pour the sorbet mixture into a suitable container and put it in the freezer for at least 4 hours. After the first 30 minutes, take it out and whisk it to break up the ice crystals, then return to the freezer. Repeat twice at half-hourly intervals. After the final whisking, stir in the stiffly beaten egg white, scoop the sorbet into the reserved watermelon shell and return it to the freezer to set firm.

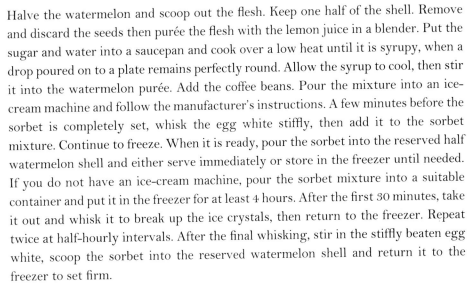

WATERMELON AND YOGURT DRINK

1 WATERMELON, ABOUT 1.2KG/2½LB
480ML/16FL OZ/2 CUPS LOW-FAT
YOGURT
240G/8OZ/1 CUP SUGAR
240ML/8FL OZ/1 CUP WATER
6 FRESH MINT SPRIGS

Scoop the flesh out of the watermelon, discard the seeds and purée the flesh in the blender. Add the yogurt, blend again to combine, then pour the mixture into a jug. In a saucepan, dissolve the sugar in the water and cook over a low heat until the liquid is syrupy when a drop poured on to a plate remains perfectly round. Allow it to cool then stir it into the watermelon mixture and add ice cubes. Pour into 6 tall glasses, decorate with the mint and serve immediately.

EXOTIC
FRUIT

BANANAS

(MUSA SAPIENTIUM)

BANANAS ARE ONE OF the most common, commercial and convenient of all fruits. Contrary to popular opinion, they do not grow on trees. The so-called banana tree is really a gigantic, fast-growing herb. This herbaceous perennial produces immense, broad leaves and drooping clusters of fruit, called 'hands', with up to two hundred upward pointing 'fingers'. Botanically these fruits are classified as berries. When the fruit has been picked the plant is cut down and from its roots another will grow and produce fruit in just eighteen months' time.

The banana originated in India and has been cultivated since ancient times in the tropics. Bananas were known in Renaissance Europe but as an exotic rarity. By the mid-nineteenth century commercial trade in bananas was developing between the United States and Hawaii, and between England and the Canary Islands.

There are two species of banana, the fruit banana, *Musa sapientium*, and the vegetable banana, *Musa paradisiaca*, called the plantain banana. A ripe plantain is green with hard, pinkish flesh and grows flatter and longer than the fruit banana. As it matures it turns darker, almost black, and softens. In its native lands the plantain is cooked as a vegetable, much like a potato, as it is high in starch and low in sugar.

There are hundreds of types of fruit bananas that are eaten fresh and also cooked in various ways, usually as desserts, as their soft, creamy flesh is sweet. Unfortunately in most markets you can only find two or three types of fruit banana, usually the common Cavendish. In Milan, I can sometimes find red bananas from Cuba or Ecuador that have creamy pink flesh and a sweet, fine flavour but I have to wait until I return to India to taste those tiny 'lady-finger' bananas.

CHICKEN BREASTS WITH BANANA AND LEEK

3 LEEKS, TRIMMED, WASHED AND
SLICED
60G/2OZ/4 TBSP UNSALTED BUTTER
6 CHICKEN BREASTS, ABOUT 180G/6OZ
EACH, SKINNED AND HALVED
LENGTHWISE
120ML/4FL OZ/½ CUP DRY WHITE WINE
SALT
3 BANANAS
1 TBSP CURRY POWDER

Sauté the leeks in the butter over a low heat for about 5 minutes or until they are translucent. Turn up the heat a little and put in the chicken breasts, then cook for 3 minutes on each side or until they are barely golden. Pour in the wine, season with salt, and cook for a few minutes over a low heat to allow the wine to evaporate. Meanwhile, peel and slice the bananas lengthwise. Add them to the chicken, heat for a couple of minutes, shaking the pan but not stirring so that the bananas do not break up. If it seems too dry, put in a little more wine, or some water. Turn off the heat, sprinkle the curry powder over and serve immediately.

BANANA AND RICE FRITTERS

600ML/1PT/2½ CUPS MILK
210G/7OZ/¾ CUP ARBORIO RICE
SALT
90G/3OZ/6 TBSP SUGAR
GRATED ZEST OF 1 LEMON
4 LARGE EGGS
PINCH POWDERED CINNAMON
3 BANANAS
120G/4OZ/1 CUP PLAIN (ALL-PURPOSE)
FLOUR
1LTR/2PT/4 CUPS OIL FOR DEEP
FRYING
2 TBSP ICING-SUGAR

Bring the milk to the boil in a saucepan, then turn down the heat, put in the rice and a pinch of salt and cook until the milk has been absorbed, stirring occasionally. Add the sugar and the lemon zest, take the pan off the heat and leave it to cool. Separate 3 of the eggs, then stir the yolks and the cinnamon into the rice. Peel and slice the bananas and stir them in too. Beat the 3 egg whites stiffly and fold them into the rice. Beat the remaining egg lightly on a plate. Spread the flour on another plate. Form the rice mixture into 36 walnut-sized balls and flatten them slightly with the back of a spoon. Dip the patties in the egg, then in the flour. Heat the oil to 170°C/350°F in a deep-fryer, or a very large saucepan, and cook the rice fritters in it, a few at a time, for about 5 minutes or until they are golden and crisp. Drain them on kitchen paper to absorb the grease and keep them warm while you finish cooking the rest. Arrange the fritters on a serving dish, dust with the icing-sugar and serve immediately. They are delicious served with crabapple wine sauce (*see page 38*).

BANANA PUDDING

3 BANANAS
JUICE OF 1 LEMON
3 LARGE EGG YOLKS
JUICE OF 1 TANGERINE
240ML/8FL OZ/1 CUP DOUBLE CREAM
120G/4OZ/½ CUP SUGAR

Preheat the oven to 175°C/350°F/gas mark 4.

Peel the bananas and purée them in a blender with the lemon juice. Pour the purée into a bowl. Beat the eggs, then add them to the banana purée. Stir in the tangerine juice a little at a time, then stir in the cream and half of the sugar. Mix well. Heat 6 individual moulds in the oven for a few minutes. Meanwhile, put the rest of the sugar into a saucepan and cook over a medium heat until it is golden, stirring from time to time. Brush each mould with the caramelized sugar, then pour in the banana mixture. Place the moulds in a bain-marie, with the water about 0.5cm (1in) deep, then bake for about 1 hour or until set. Take them out of the oven and allow them to cool a little. To turn them out, slide a knife around the edge of each pudding, invert it over a serving dish and shake. Serve warm or at room temperature.

KIWIS

(ACTINIDIA CHINENSIS)

THIS GENERATION OF EUROPEANS might be forgiven for thinking of the kiwi as a Mediterranean fruit, so omnipresent has it become in our markets and on our tables. It is cultivated commercially in Italy on a vast scale, especially in Puglia. However, the kiwi originally came from China and was known for years as the Chinese gooseberry. At the beginning of the twentieth century New Zealand began to experiment with seeds from China and now exports vast quantities of the fruit.

The kiwi plant is a vigorous climbing vine that requires strong support for its branches. It blossoms in large pale yellow flowers and bears a furry brown fruit the size and shape of a large egg and as curious in aspect as the little flightless bird for which it is named. At first sight the French thought these unassuming little fruits so quaint-looking they called them *souris vegetalis*, vegetable mice.

The fuzzy brown skin hides a beautiful, clear, bright green fruit with tiny black seeds arranged around a white core. The flesh is juicy and soft and intensely perfumed with a delicately sweet and slightly acidic flavour all its own. It reminds me most of strawberries.

In the eighties the kiwi was the darling of the *nouvelle cuisine* and appeared everywhere, in salads and soups, with fish, roasts and desserts. Perhaps because of that overuse, it still surprises me how delicious a kiwi can be. Now that the hype is over, I use them often for colour and flavour in any number of dishes. The flesh is also useful as a marinade to tenderize meat.

CHICKEN WITH KIWI

1 CHICKEN, ABOUT 1.5KG/3LB
1 HANDFUL FRESH BAY LEAVES, OR
3 DRIED
30G/1OZ/2 TBSP UNSALTED BUTTER
2 TBSP EXTRA-VIRGIN OLIVE OIL
SALT AND PEPPER
60ML/2FL OZ/¼ CUP DRY WHITE WINE
6 KIWIS, PEELED AND DICED

Preheat the oven to 175°C/350°F/gas mark 4.

Fill the chicken cavity with the bay leaves. Put the bird in a baking-dish, smear the butter and oil over the breast and legs and season with salt and pepper. Roast for about 90 minutes, then take it out of the oven, pour in the wine, add the kiwis and put it back for 5 minutes. To serve, carve the chicken and arrange it on a serving platter. Surround it with the kiwis, then pour over the cooking juices.

KIWI PARFAIT

MAKES APPROXIMATELY 1 LITRE/
1¾ PINTS
4 LARGE EGG YOLKS
120G/4OZ/½ CUP SUGAR
480ML/16FL OZ/2 CUPS MILK
15G/½OZ GELATINE LEAVES OR
CRYSTALS
8 KIWIS, PEELED
60ML/2FL OZ/¼ CUP DOUBLE
(HEAVY) CREAM

Beat together the egg yolks and the sugar. Stir in the milk and pour into the top half of a double-boiler, or set the mixing bowl over a pan of simmering water, and cook, stirring continuously, over a low heat until the custard thickens and coats the back of the spoon. Do not let it boil. Meanwhile put the gelatine leaves in a bowl, cover them with water and leave them to soak for 10 minutes or dissolve the crystals following the instructions on the package. Drain, squeeze out the excess liquid then stir the gelatine into the custard, off the heat, until it has dissolved. Leave it to cool.

Purée 6 of the kiwis in the blender. Stir the cream into the custard, then the puréed kiwis. Wet a 1-litre (2pt) bowl, then pour in the parfait mixture and leave it to set in the refrigerator for about 3 hours.

To turn it out, slide the point of a knife around the edge of the bowl to loosen the parfait, then invert it on to a platter and shake. Slice the remaining 2 kiwis and use them to decorate it. Replace the parfait in the refrigerator until you are ready to serve.

KIWI AND RICOTTA MOUSSE

6 KIWIS, PEELED
480G/16OZ FRESH RICOTTA
120G/4OZ/½ CUP SUGAR
60ML/2FL OZ/¼ CUP DOUBLE
(HEAVY) CREAM

Purée 4 of the kiwis in the blender. Beat the ricotta in a bowl with the kiwi purée and the sugar until smooth. Whisk the cream until it forms soft peaks, then fold it into the ricotta mixture. Pour the mousse mixture into a serving bowl. Slice the remaining 2 kiwis and use them to decorate the mousse, then put it into the refrigerator to chill for about 2 hours.

LIMES

(CITRUS AURANTIFOLIA)

'...in this bower,
This little lime-tree bower,'
(COLERIDGE, THIS LIME-TREE BOWER MY PRISON, 1797)

IF YOU WERE TO LOOK UP 'lime' in an English-Italian dictionary, you would find *limetta* or *lima* or *limonebergamotto* or just plain lime. The truth is that Italians do not really know what to call a lime as it does not exist in Italy. Years ago when I was in Florida and had eaten a delicious piece of Key Lime Pie, I was certain I would be able to duplicate the recipe at home, although I had never seen limes in the market. Well, sadly, I discovered that these natives of the tropics are not hardy enough for the Mediterranean, even Sicily, where they have tried to cultivate them. However, they are readily available in Britain from large supermarkets.

Limes are the smallest of citrus fruit, round or oval in shape, with smooth skin that is bright green when harvested but turns yellow when fully ripe. They are highly aromatic and have juicy flesh that tastes sharper yet less sour than most lemons. They might resemble lemons but the fragrance and the tanginess of limes are unique.

Only two types of true lime tree exist. The Mexican lime can only be grown in mild climates. Its small fruit is also known as the 'bartender's lime' because of its popularity in cocktails. The Tahitian lime tree is less delicate than the Mexican and produces larger, juicier fruit. Of course, tropical limes are not related to the ornamental European tree, sometimes called a lime but which is really the linden.

English sailors were given lime juice to prevent scurvy, which was caused by a lack of vitamin C in a diet that consisted almost exclusively of preserved foods. Rum was added to preserve the lime juice, which is what gave me the idea for lime punch. Limes and lemons are interchangeable in most recipes but remember that less lime is required. Like lemon, lime brings out the flavour of other ingredients.

LIME PUNCH

60G/2OZ CLOVES
2 LIMES
1½ LITRES/3PT/6 CUPS STRONG TEA
PINCH POWDERED CINNAMON
240ML/8FL OZ/1 CUP RUM
180G/6OZ/¾ CUP SUGAR

Preheat the oven to 175°C/350°F/gas mark 4.

Stick the cloves into the limes, then bake them for about 20 minutes. Bring the tea to the boil. Put the hot limes into a metal bowl, then pour over the tea and add the cinnamon. Bring the rum to the boil with the sugar, then, away from heat, set fire to it. Pour it, still flaming, on to the tea and serve immediately.

LIME APPLE CAKE

2 LARGE EGGS
120G/4OZ/½ CUP SUGAR
120G/4OZ/1 CUP PLAIN (ALL-PURPOSE)
FLOUR, PLUS EXTRA FOR DUSTING
120G/4OZ/8 TBSP UNSALTED BUTTER,
MELTED, PLUS EXTRA FOR GREASING
GRATED ZEST AND JUICE OF 3 LIMES
1 TBSP BAKING POWDER
3 LARGE COOKING APPLES
DOUBLE (HEAVY) CREAM, TO SERVE

Preheat the oven to 175°C/350°F/gas mark 4.

Beat together the eggs and the sugar in a mixing bowl. Incorporate the flour a little at a time, whisking carefully. Beat in the butter, the lime zest and juice and finally the baking powder. The mixture should be quite loose. Now peel and core the apples, slice them thinly and stir them into the cake mixture. Butter and flour a 23-cm (9in) springform cake tin. Fill it with the mixture, level the top and bake for 40 minutes. Then remove it from the oven, cover the surface with foil and return it to the oven for another 20 minutes. Take it out of the oven, remove the foil and let the cake cool a little. Then open the springform and turn it out. Serve warm or at room temperature with double cream.

LIME AND RHUBARB CREAM

900G/1LB 14OZ RHUBARB
JUICE OF 3 LIMES
120G/4OZ/½ CUP SUGAR
240ML/8FL OZ/1 CUP DOUBLE
(HEAVY) CREAM

Peel the rhubarb and throw away any leaves, which are poisonous. Cut the stalks into short lengths and put them into a saucepan with the lime juice. Cover the pan and cook over a low heat until the rhubarb is very tender, about 30 minutes, stirring occasionally. Towards the end of the cooking time, if there seems to be too much liquid, take off the lid and let it evaporate. Pass the rhubarb through a food mill, or process it in a blender or food processor, then stir in the sugar. Let it cool. Beat the cream stiffly, then fold it into the rhubarb. Divide the lime and rhubarb cream between 6 champagne flutes and leave it in the refrigerator to chill.

MANGOES

(MANGIFERA INDICA)

FOR MY GENERATION mangoes were *the* exotic fruit and for many their reputation still holds, even in the midst of competition from dozens of other tropical fruits now available on the world market. I think the mango has the most deliciously distinctive taste of all, reminiscent of a flowery peach. They have been called the 'peach of the tropics'.

India is the native land of the mango, where it has flourished for several thousand years. Colonialists brought them to the West Indies, Africa and other tropical lands. Now over two thousand varieties are cultivated, even in California and Florida. For me, however, this ambrosial fruit will always be associated with the sensuality of India.

The Indian mango tree, which provided shade for Buddha, is an evergreen that grows to great heights. It is topped with a crown of dense, narrow leaves that cascade to the ground. Long sprays of yellowish-red flowers blossom in large clusters at the end of each branch, hundreds in each bunch. The fruit dangles temptingly from long stems. When ripe most mangoes turn golden. Some types remain yellow-green, while others vary from pink to bright red. The reddish-yellow flesh is soft and moist. Certain varieties are fibrous, but the popular ones you are likely to find at the market have a creamy consistency. Their flavour is sweet with a pleasingly acidic aftertaste.

That's the good news. The bad news is that mangoes are notoriously clingstone and clingpeel, which means that they are difficult to peel and getting to their succulent flesh is hard work. Every cook has her method for best liberating this fruit. I can only recommend patience and perseverance with a paring knife. The end result is certainly worth the effort. Whenever I am served a peeled and prepared fresh mango, I appreciate the tender loving care that has been dedicated to my pleasure.

MANGO AND PROSCIUTTO SKEWERS

3 MANGOES, PEELED AND STONED
18 PAPER-THIN SLICES PROSCIUTTO
(PARMA HAM)

Slice each mango into 6 pieces. Fold each slice of prosciutto and thread on to wooden skewers or cocktail sticks, alternating with pieces of mango. As an alternative, use pineapple instead of the mango, or serve a selection of both.

MANGO AND MINT SHERBET

1.5KG/3LB MANGOES, PEELED AND
STONED
240G/8OZ/1 CUP SUGAR
120ML/4FL OZ/½ CUP WATER
1 HANDFUL FRESH MINT LEAVES
60ML/2FL OZ/¼ CUP VIN SANTO OR
SAUTERNE

Purée the mango flesh in a blender. Put the sugar into a saucepan with the water and mint and cook over a low heat until the liquid is syrupy – a drop poured on to a plate will remain perfectly round and firm. Discard the mint and let the syrup cool. Then stir the syrup and the wine into the mango purée, then pour it into an ice-cream machine and continue according to the manufacturer's instructions. If you do not have an ice-cream machine, pour the sherbet mixture into a suitable container and put it into the freezer for at least 4 hours. After the first 30 minutes, take it out and whisk it to break up the ice crystals, then return it to the freezer. Whisk twice more at half-hourly intervals, then leave it in the freezer to firm. To serve, scoop into wine-glasses with a little more wine poured over, if you like.

FRIED CHICKEN BREASTS WITH MANGO SAUCE

240G/8OZ/1 CUP CHOPPED ALMONDS
1 LARGE EGG
240G/8OZ/1 CUP FINE DRY
BREADCRUMBS
6 CHICKEN BREASTS, SKINNED AND
TRIMMED
90G/3OZ/6 TBSP UNSALTED BUTTER
3 TBSP EXTRA-VIRGIN OLIVE OIL
2 MANGOES, PEELED AND STONED
JUICE OF 1 LEMON
1 TBSP CURRY POWDER
SALT

Preheat the oven to 175°F/350°C/gas mark 4.

Toast the almonds in the oven for about 10 minutes or until they are golden. Don't allow them to brown or they will be bitter. Beat the egg lightly on a deep plate with a little salt. Spread the breadcrumbs on another plate. Dip the chicken breasts in the egg, then coat them with the breadcrumbs. Heat the butter and the oil in a frying-pan, put in the chicken and cook for about 3 minutes on each side, or until it is barely golden. Drain on kitchen paper and reserve. Purée the mangoes in a blender, add the lemon juice and blend again briefly. Pour the mango purée into a pan and heat it. Add the chicken breasts, cover the pan, and cook for 10 more minutes, turning once, over a low heat to allow the flavours to blend. Sprinkle the curry powder over, season with salt and serve immediately.

GUAVAS

(PSIDIUM GUAYAVA)

WHEN I WANT TO BUY GUAVAS, and other rare, exotic fruit, I head straight for Peck in the centre of Milan, not far from the Piazza del Duomo, one of the most splendid food emporiums in Italy – and all of Europe, for that matter. It comprises several different shops on two adjoining streets, with every delicious food you can imagine, from salami, cheeses and fresh pasta to breads, desserts and wines. In the midst of this sensual feast, there is no problem locating the guavas in the greengrocery section. Their unmistakable, fabulous scent fills the air with a rich floral bouquet, similar to but even more intense than quince. When I cook them, their aroma is even more amazing, perfuming all the rooms in the house.

Guavas are native to Brazil and are commercially raised in most warm, tropical countries. Attempts have been made to cultivate them even in Florida and California. They grow on evergreen shrubs or small trees that blossom in fragrant white flowers. Depending on the variety, the fruit is shaped like a plum, a fig or small pear. A large type, called the supreme, is the size of a peach. Tropical guavas have thin, greenish-yellow skin, and flesh that varies from white to pale pink with a meaty and pleasingly gritty texture. The ancient Indians of Mexico called it the 'sand plum'. They have a sweet, honeyed flavour, slightly acidic. The seeds in some types are soft and can be swallowed along with the flesh. The strawberry guava (*Psidium cattleianum*) bears small round fruits that turn red to dark purple when ripe and have an intense flavour.

Good guavas can be eaten fresh from the fruit bowl and add colour and flavour to salads. Because of their creamy consistency when cooked, I find them especially suited to sweet and savoury sauces.

GUAVA SAUTEED WITH CHIVES

3 GUAVAS, SEEDED AND SLICED
30G/1OZ/2 TBSP UNSALTED BUTTER
SALT
180ML/6FL OZ/⅔ CUP DOUBLE
(HEAVY) CREAM
1 TBSP SWEET PAPRIKA
2 TBSP FINELY CHOPPED CHIVES

Sauté the guava slices in the butter over a low heat for a few minutes to warm them through. Add a pinch of salt and the cream, then cook for a couple of minutes until the sauce thickens slightly. Sprinkle over the paprika, then the chives, and serve immediately. This makes an excellent accompaniment for spicy Mexican dishes.

GUAVA ICE-CREAM

MAKES APPROXIMATELY 1 LITRE/
1¾ PINTS
6 GUAVAS, PEELED, SEEDED AND DICED
480ML/16FL OZ/2 CUPS DOUBLE
(HEAVY) CREAM
240G/8OZ/1 CUP SUGAR
2 TBSP KIRSCH

Purée the guavas in a blender. Heat the cream, do not let it boil, and dissolve the sugar in it. Allow it to cool, then stir it into the guava purée with the Kirsch. Pour the mixture into an ice-cream machine and follow the manufacturer's instructions. If you do not have a machine, pour the mixture into a suitable container and put it into the freezer for at least 4 hours. After the first 30 minutes take it out and whisk it to break up the ice crystals, then return to the freezer. Whisk twice more at half-hourly intervals, then leave the ice-cream in the freezer to firm up.

GUAVA SAUCE

2 GUAVAS, PEELED, SEEDED AND DICED
90G/3OZ/6 TBSP UNSALTED BUTTER
1 TSP CHILLI POWDER

Purée the guavas in a blender. Melt the butter and stir it into the guava pulp with the chilli powder. Pour the sauce into a bowl and serve it with boiled or roasted ham.

LYCHEES

(LITCHI CHINENSIS)

At school we read the story of a 'Chinese princess', the Emperor's favourite concubine, for whom he had fresh lychees brought hundreds of miles from Canton to the palace every day by horseback just to give her pleasure. I wondered what was so special about fresh lychees. Years later, in China, I found out.

Lychees are a most ancient and noble Chinese fruit that grow on a splendidly grand ornamental evergreen tree with beautiful coppery leaves. After long cultivation it eventually produces brightly coloured bunches of pinkish-red fruit that look like large strawberries. It reminds me of the corbezzolo, the arbus or strawberry tree, which grows in my garden at Coltibuono.

The delicate flesh of the lychee is protected by a crisp shell. When this husk is cracked away, a greyish white giant 'pearl' is revealed, in the centre of which is a glossy mahogany-coloured stone. The peeled, translucent fruit is often likened to a peeled grape. In her book, *Uncommon Fruits and Vegetables*, Elizabeth Schneider described it best, as looking 'more like a sea creature than a fruit'. You are not likely to forget eating your first fresh lychee. The texture is fibrous and the consistency slightly chewy. The fresh lychees I have eaten have had a somewhat musky scent, reminiscent of roses and a juicy, sweet taste.

In Italy I can buy fresh lychees in midwinter. Served just as they are with a fine dessert wine, they will liven up the end of a meal. You can also buy dried lychees sometimes called 'Chinese nuts'. These are often used in Oriental sweet and sour dishes.

Thinking back on that story from my childhood, I suspect the ancient Chinese also considered lychees an aphrodisiac, which would help to explain what all that fuss was about.

SWEET AND SOUR FISH WITH LYCHEES

90ML/3FL OZ/6 TBSP EXTRA-VIRGIN
OLIVE OIL
60ML/2FL OZ/¼ CUP WHITE WINE
VINEGAR
2 TBSP SUGAR
60ML/2FL OZ/¼ CUP DRY WHITE WINE
3 TBSP SOY SAUCE
2 TBSP CORNFLOUR
4 TBSP WATER
1 SMALL ONION, PEELED AND CHOPPED
6 COD STEAKS, ABOUT 210G/7OZ EACH
1.5KG/3LB LYCHEES, PEELED AND
STONED
SALT

Warm 2 tablespoons of the oil over a low heat. Add the vinegar, sugar, white wine and soy sauce. Meanwhile, blend together the cornflour and the water until the mixture is smooth. Add it to the sauce, cook until it thickens and coats the back of a spoon, then set it aside. In another pan, heat the rest of the oil, put in the onion and cook for 3 minutes until it is translucent, then put in the cod and cook over a medium heat until it is just golden. Pour in the sauce, add the lychees and season carefully – the soy sauce is salty. Cover the pan and cook over a low heat for a few minutes to allow the flavours to blend and the lychees to warm through. Serve immediately.

LYCHEES IN A WATERMELON CUP WITH CARAMELIZED ORANGE PEEL

1 WATERMELON, ABOUT 2KG/4½LB
120ML/4FL OZ/½ CUP MEDIUM SHERRY
1KG/2¼ LB LYCHEES, PEELED AND
STONED
2 ORANGES
120G/4OZ/½ CUP SUGAR
4 TBSP WATER
1 TBSP LEMON JUICE
1 TBSP ALMOND OIL

Cut the top off the watermelon and remove the flesh with a sharp knife. Reserve the shell. Remove and discard the seeds, then either dice the flesh or make it into balls with a melon-baller. Put the diced flesh with the sherry into the watermelon shell. Add the lychees and mix carefully. Put the fruit into the refrigerator to chill for at least 2 hours. Meanwhile peel the oranges thinly, discarding the pith, then cut the peel into thin strips. Put the sugar and the water into a saucepan, bring it to the boil, add the orange peel and lemon juice, and cook until the syrup begins to caramelize. Brush a flat surface with the oil. Remove the orange peel from the syrup and lay it on the oiled surface. Let it cool, then scatter it over the fruit and serve immediately.

LYCHEES WITH STRAWBERRY SAUCE

1KG/2¼LB LYCHEES, PEELED AND
STONED
300G/10OZ FRESH STRAWBERRIES
3 TBSP HONEY

Put the lychees into a serving bowl. Purée the strawberries in a blender, then add the honey and blend again briefly. Pour the strawberry sauce over the lychees and refrigerate until you are ready to serve.

PAPAYAS

(CARICA PAPAYA)

RECENTLY I READ that scientists studying plant genetics have discovered that the exotic papaya is first cousin to the garden cabbage. This would certainly have come as a shock to Linnaeus, the eighteenth-century botanist who first established a universal system to define plants by genus and species. Although the news also surprised me, I did know from my travels in India that the papaya is often treated as a vegetable, like squash.

Originally from Malaysia, these large, tropical fruits only became commercially viable in the mid-twentieth century, when a variety called Solo was developed in Hawaii. As its name implies, it grows to a size suitable for one person. Now papaya are cultivated in Asia, Africa, South America and Florida as well as Hawaii, and can be found on the market all year round.

The fruit grows in clusters on a giant, prolific plant. Depending on the variety, the papaya may be shaped like an avocado, a banana or more commonly a pear, and varies in colour when ripe from yellowish green to deep yellow. It has creamy orange flesh and a central cavity filled with dozens of black seeds. The taste is sweet and refreshing.

Because the papaya is 88 per cent water, it is usually eaten raw in tropical climates, as a thirst-quencher. In many ways, the papaya is very much like a melon and can be used in much the same way. In fact, in times past the papaya was often referred to as a tree melon.

PAPAYA RISOTTO

2 LITRES/3½PT/8 CUPS CHICKEN STOCK
60G/2OZ/4 TBSP UNSALTED BUTTER
600G/1¼LB/2½ CUPS ARBORIO RICE
1 PAPAYA, PEELED, SEEDED AND DICED
SALT AND PEPPER
1 QUARTER-BOTTLE CHAMPAGNE

Put a large serving dish to warm in the oven. In a pan, bring the stock to the boil, then reduce the heat. Melt the butter in another saucepan, put in the rice and cook over a medium heat, stirring, for about 3 minutes or until the rice is hot. Pour in enough of the boiling stock to cover the rice and cook, stirring all the time, adding more stock to keep the rice constantly covered. Never let the stock be completely absorbed. The rice should be cooked in about 15 minutes from when you started to add the stock. Now stir in the papaya and turn off the heat. Check the seasoning and adjust with salt and pepper. The consistency of the risotto should be creamy. Cover the pan and leave it to stand for 2 minutes. Remove the wire from the champagne bottle. Pour the rice into the serving dish and place the champagne bottle in the centre. The cork will pop out and the champagne will flow over the rice. Remove the bottle, stir and serve immediately.

FILLET STEAK WITH PAPAYA

90G/3OZ/6 TBSP UNSALTED BUTTER
1 TBSP PAPRIKA
1 PAPAYA, PEELED AND SEEDED
6 FILLET STEAKS, ABOUT 210G/7OZ
EACH
6 PAPER-THIN RASHERS SMOKED
BACON
2 TBSP EXTRA-VIRGIN OLIVE OIL
SALT

Beat 2 tablespoons of the butter with the paprika and put it into the refrigerator to chill. Slice the papaya crossways into 6 pieces, then set it aside. Wrap each fillet steak in a rasher of bacon. Heat the rest of the butter and the oil in a frying-pan, put in the steaks and cook over a high heat for about 3 minutes on each side, if you wish them to be rare, or a little longer if you prefer. Season, then lay them on a warm serving platter. Put the papaya slices into the pan in which the steaks were cooked and heat them for 1 minute on each side. Lay a slice on each steak. Divide the paprika butter into 6, lay a piece on each papaya slice and serve.

PAPAYA SORBET

MAKES APPROXIMATELY 1 LITRE/1¾PT
4 PAPAYAS, PEELED AND SEEDED
JUICE OF 3 LIMES
180G/6OZ/⅞ CUP SUGAR
240ML/8FL OZ/1 CUP WATER

Purée the papayas in a blender, add the lime juice, blend again, and set aside. Put the sugar and water into a saucepan, bring to the boil, then cook over a low heat until it is syrupy – a drop poured on to a plate will stay perfectly round. Allow it to cool, then add it to the papaya purée. Pour the mixture into an ice-cream maker, then follow the manufacturer's instructions. If you do not have an ice-cream machine, pour the sorbet mixture into a container and put it in the freezer for at least 4 hours. After the first 30 minutes take it out and whisk it, then return it to the freezer. Whisk twice more at half-hourly intervals, then leave the sorbet in the freezer until it is firm.

PINEAPPLES

(ANANASSA SATIVA)

'Standing by his Majesty at dinner in the Presence,
there was that rare fruit called the King Pine,
growing in Barbadoes and the West Indies,
the first of them I have ever seene.'

(EVELYN'S DIARY, 1668, QUOTED IN BUNYARD)

ITALIANS USUALLY PREFER to end a meal with fruit rather than a pudding. On a grand occasion in the winter, restaurants might serve each guest with half of a fresh pineapple cut lengthwise, its plume of green leaves still attached, the succulent, fragrant flesh diced into bite-sized cubes and left in the shell.

Pineapples were first seen by European explorers in Brazil, where they are native. They referred to this extraordinary fruit by its local Indian name, ananas. It created quite a stir in eighteenth-century England and the landed gentry began to grow them in their hot-houses. They called the fruit pineapple, because of its resemblance to a large pine cone. The pineapple became a favourite fruit of Louis XV. It remained a rare and expensive fruit right through the nineteenth century until the time of modern commercial pineapple plantations. Probably because pineapples were so rare and precious, English landowners began to place large pineapples carved in stone on top of the entrance gates to their estates – a decorative symbol, one would imagine, of the generous hospitality that awaited the guest within, which might also have included a taste of the real thing. Now it is a commonplace fruit, at least in its canned forms and as juice, but a fresh, ripe pineapple still has something exotic about it, and familiarity has not diminished its delicious taste.

The pineapple is an 'aggregate' fruit. Each of those distinctive segments on its tough skin is an individual fruit, the product of a single flower. I am told there are hundreds of varieties of pineapple, although we see just one in Italy, with an occasional sighting of a baby or miniature one.

When warmed, pineapple seems even more fragrant and sweet and complements both sweet and savoury dishes. Nutritionists confirm what the appetite has always instinctively known: the pineapple contains an enzyme that aids digestion, making it a perfect fruit to conclude a meal.

PINEAPPLE AND HAM SALAD

FOR THE MAYONNAISE
1 LARGE EGG YOLK
SALT
90G/3FL OZ/6 TBSP EXTRA-VIRGIN
OLIVE OIL
JUICE OF ½ LEMON
2 TBSP MILK

FOR THE SALAD
1 COS LETTUCE, ABOUT 300G/10OZ,
OUTSIDE LEAVES REMOVED
1 PINEAPPLE, ABOUT 1KG/2½LB,
PEELED, CORED, TRIMMED AND DICED
300G/10OZ PARMA OR SERRANO HAM,
THINLY SLICED

Make the mayonnaise: with a wooden spoon beat the egg yolk in a bowl with a little salt, then beat in the oil a drop at a time. Using a circular motion stir in lemon juice to taste and milk to thin it a little.

Line a large salad bowl with the lettuce leaves. Toss together the pineapple and the ham and spoon it on top of the lettuce. Pour over the mayonnaise and serve. You can keep the salad in the refrigerator for a few hours, but allow it to return to room temperature before serving.

154

PINEAPPLE AND CHOCOLATE MOUSSE

180G/6OZ BITTER CHOCOLATE
90G/3OZ/6 TBSP UNSALTED BUTTER,
PLUS EXTRA FOR GREASING.
4 LARGE EGGS, SEPARATED
120G/4OZ/½ CUP SUGAR
30G/1OZ/2 TBSP PLAIN (ALL-PURPOSE)
FLOUR
1 PINEAPPLE, ABOUT 1KG/2¼LB,
PEELED, CORED, TRIMMED AND SLICED
INTO 6

Preheat the oven to 200°C/400°F/gas mark 6.

Place the chocolate and the butter in the top half of a double-boiler, or into a mixing bowl set over a pan of simmering water, and allow it to melt over a low heat. Stir well, then let it cool. Beat the egg yolks with the sugar and the flour, then stir in the chocolate mixture. Beat the egg whites until just stiff and fold into the chocolate mixture. Butter a 23-cm (9-in) soufflé dish and lay 3 pineapple slices on the bottom. Fill with half the chocolate cream and the rest of the pineapple. Fill with the rest of the cream and cook in the oven for about 30 minutes. Serve immediately while it is puffed up or later at room temperature, in which case it will become more like a soft torte.

PINEAPPLE CAKE

120G/4OZ/1 CUP PLAIN (ALL-PURPOSE)
FLOUR, PLUS EXTRA FOR DUSTING
15G/½OZ BAKING POWDER
2 LARGE EGGS
120G/4OZ/½ CUP SUGAR
120G/4OZ/8 TBSP UNSALTED BUTTER,
MELTED, PLUS A LITTLE EXTRA
1 PINEAPPLE, ABOUT 1.5KG/3LB,
PEELED, CORED, CUT INTO WEDGES
AND DICED

Preheat the oven to 175°C/350°F/gas mark 4.

Butter a 23-cm (9-in) springform cake tin and dust it with flour, then tip out the excess. Sift the flour and the baking powder into a mixing bowl, then stir in the eggs thoroughly so that there are no lumps. Now add the sugar and finally the melted butter. Mix well to form a smooth batter. Stir in the pineapple and pour into the prepared cake tin. Bake for 40 minutes, then take it out of the oven, cover the top with foil and return to the oven for another 20 minutes. Take it out, leave it to cool in the tin, then unclip the springform and turn out the cake on to a plate. Serve it either warm or at room temperature, perhaps with a little icing-sugar dusted over the top or with thick cream.

POMEGRANATES

(PUNICA GRANATUM)

'My ripe figs and rich pomegranates,
In infant joy at they feet,
O Urizon!
(William Blake, The Book of Ahania, 1795)

In one of her splendid still-life paintings, the seventeenth-century Italian artist Giovanna Garzoni depicts a single pomegranate sitting in a bed of dried leaves on a heavy marble plate. The apple-shaped form of the leathery-skinned, reddish-gold fruit is split into three sections, exposing multitudinous white seeds, each encased in a translucent sac of carmine-coloured jelly. The only other objects in the painting are a snail, two chestnuts and an almost transparent grasshopper-like insect. I read them as symbols of death and rebirth, for that has been the universal significance of the pomegranate for thousands of years, beginning with the ancient Persians. Paintings of pomegranates decorated classical Greek tombs, as well as medieval and Renaissance Christian art.

The eighteenth-century writer Giacomo Castelvetro remarks of pomegranates that they are good eaten on their own or used as seasoning for cooked dishes, and as a restorative for invalids. 'The juice assuages the violent thirst of the feverish. We make a beautiful-looking wine from its pretty seeds for that purpose.'

Unfortunately the pomegranate seems to have lost some of its gastronomic appeal in contemporary times, at least in the Western world. Maybe this is because it is so time-consuming to prepare. I can think of only two ways one is likely to taste pomegranates today in regional Italian cooking. One comes from Vicenza in the region of the Veneto, *paeta rosta al melgaragno*, roast turkey with pomegranate juice. The other is in a refreshing Sicilian *granita*, sweetened pomegranate juice poured over crushed ice.

For children (they like to play with pomegranates in the kitchen and with a little direction will happily spoon out the seeds for you) or those with time and patience, this fruit will add its wonderful ruby colour, crunchy texture and sweet-sour flavour to all sorts of dishes, rice, fish, fowl, meats and desserts.

SOLE WITH POMEGRANATES

6 LARGE SOLE FILLETS, ABOUT
210G/7OZ EACH, TRIMMED
3 TBSP PLAIN (ALL-PURPOSE) FLOUR
60G/2OZ/4 TBSP UNSALTED BUTTER
2 POMEGRANATES, HALVED, SEEDS
REMOVED, PITH DISCARDED
60ML/2FL OZ/¼ CUP DRY WHITE WINE
SALT AND PEPPER

Dust the sole fillets with the flour. Heat the butter in a frying-pan, then sauté the sole over a medium heat until just turning golden. Scatter in the pomegranate seeds, pour over the wine, season with salt and pepper, cover and cook for 1 minute. Turn the fillets and cook, uncovered, for 1 more minute. Serve immediately.

POMEGRANATES WITH CARDOON

1 LARGE CARDOON, ABOUT 1.5KG/3LB
30G/1OZ/2 TBSP PLAIN (ALL-PURPOSE)
FLOUR
3 TBSP EXTRA-VIRGIN OLIVE OIL
1 SMALL WHITE ONION, PEELED AND
CHOPPED
480G/1LB RIPE PLUM TOMATOES OR
TINNED PLUM TOMATOES, WITH JUICE
SALT AND PEPPER
3 POMEGRANATES, HALVED, SEEDS
REMOVED, PITH DISCARDED
120ML/4FL OZ/½ CUP YOGURT

Have ready a bowl of acidulated water.

Separate the cardoon stalks, remove the stringy bits, trim the stalks and cut them into 2.5-cm (1in) lengths. Put them into the bowl of acidulated water while you bring a saucepan of water to the boil. Put in the cardoon, sprinkle over the flour and cook for around 10 minutes. (The flour will prevent the cardoon discolouring.) Drain and reserve. Heat the oil in a frying-pan, put in the onion and cook over a low heat for about 3 minutes or until it is translucent, stirring occasionally. Bring another saucepan of water to the boil. Turn off the heat, plunge in the (fresh) tomatoes, leave them for 30 seconds, then drain, peel and dice them. If you are using tinned tomatoes, you need only chop them. Add the cardoon to the onions and sauté for about 5 minutes, stirring occasionally. Then put in the tomatoes, season with salt and pepper and continue to cook until the juice has evaporated – about 5 more minutes. Turn off the heat, scatter in the pomegranate seeds, stir in the yogurt and cover the pan. Leave it to stand for 2 minutes, then serve.

POMEGRANATE COCKTAIL

6 POMEGRANATES, SEEDS REMOVED
AND JUICED
300ML/10FL OZ/2¼ CUPS WHITE RUM
300ML/10FL OZ/2¼ CUPS SODA WATER
3 TSP SUGAR
6 ORANGE SLICES
ICE CUBES

Strain the pomegranate juice, then pour it into a jug with the rum, the soda water and the sugar. Mix well, then pour into 6 tall glasses over ice cubes. Decorate with the orange slices and serve immediately.

ACKNOWLEDGEMENTS

Mike Newton would like to thank the following
individuals and organisations for their assistance
in the photography for this book:

Ruth Prentice and Susan Berry for their help
with, and enthusiasm for, the original project.

Gabrielle Townsend for her invaluable advice
and encouragement.

Jeanette and Graham at Tableprops, London, for
providing props and backgrounds.

For help with supplying fruit, flowers and leaves
for photography:
The Brogdale Trust, Faversham, Kent
Pantiles Nursery, Chertsey, Surrey
The Citrus Centre, Pulborough, West Sussex
Veneta Bullen
David Roche, Rupert Street Market, London

Colin Webb, Vivien James and Clare Johnson at
Pavilion Books.

David Fordham for his design.